SWIMMING HOLES

of Washington

ANNA KATZ &
SHANE ROBINSON

SWIMMING HOLES
of Washington

Perfect places to play

SKIPSTONE

Copyright © 2018 by Anna Katz and Shane Robinson

Published by Skipstone, an imprint of Mountaineers Books
Skipstone and its colophons are registered trademarks of Mountaineers Books.

Printed in China
First edition, 2018

Copyeditor: Kris Fulsaas
Design: Heidi Smets
Cartographer: Pease Press
Cover photograph: Top: iStock/Goami; Bottom: *Methow River at Mazama (Swim #61)*
Back cover photograph: *Falls Creek/Lazy Bear Falls (Swim 58)*
All photos by the authors unless credited otherwise.

Library of Congress Cataloging-in-Publication Data is on file

ISBN (paperback): 978-1-59485-999-1
ISBN (ebook): 978-1-68051-000-3

Printed on FSC-certified materials.

Skipstone books may be purchased for corporate, educational, or other promotional sales, and our authors are available for a wide range of events. For information on special discounts or booking an author, contact our customer service at 800.553.4453 or mbooks@mountaineersbooks.org.

Skipstone
1001 SW Klickitat Way, Suite 201
Seattle, Washington 98134
206.223.6303
www.skipstonebooks.org
www.mountaineersbooks.org

LIVE LIFE. MAKE RIPPLES.

For our parents, Paul Burstein and Florence Katz
Burstein and George and Julie Robinson:
thanks for teaching us to swim

CONTENTS

Summer vibes at Dougan Falls (Swim #1)

INTRODUCTION

WASHINGTON STATE IS HOME to more than 8000 lakes and approximately 70,439 miles of river. Most of these rivers are named for the Native American tribes that lived on their banks: the Klickitat, Cowlitz, Chehalis, the Wenatchee, and Skagit, to name just a few (see sidebar). Water is everywhere in Washington, whether it's saltwater providing a port to a city, freshwater flowing through a valley, or rain falling from the sky.

The Pacific Northwest attracts, along with techies and coffee drinkers and musicians, many die-hard outdoorspeople who are determined to be outside, no matter the weather. We won't let the rain—nor seasonal affective disorder or urban living—stop us. To that end, we drive up into the mountains to ski and snowboard, ride commuter bikes in downpours, and hike on dripping, mossy trails despite howling wind.

Many people get outside, rain or shine . . . or rain. But, to generalize, everyone here lives for the summer, and for good reason: summertime in this region is absolute paradise. Many a tourist has decided to move here after visiting in July or August. From late June through September, depending on the year, the sky is a boundless blue, the grass stays green, the temperature is happy-place ideal, and there's always some gorgeous body of water to swim in wherever you happen to be.

We like to swim, and a few years ago, we were looking for a guidebook to swimming holes in the Pacific Northwest. Many wonderful books mention swimming holes or explore hot springs but, by George, we couldn't find any whose sole mission was to specifically educate and direct us to swimming holes. So we decided to write our own.

For us, swimming in these outdoor locales is not simply a hobby—it is a lifestyle and a philosophy. It's not about swimming laps or burning calories; we want to be out in the natural environment and to play like the fish, otters, and whales that are our close relations. We are in it to have a good time. We want to live slow.

With this philosophy in mind, we wrote this simple guidebook that could live in the glove box of your family's minivan, on the coffee table next to your roommate's oversize glasses and empty can of PBR, or in the pocket of your hard-core-trekker's backpack along with the gorp. This book is for parents who want a nice place to safely entertain their kids while spending a day in the water. It's for outdoor recreationists who are looking for an activity when the ski slopes are closed or the weather's too hot for a climb—and maybe for those who want to jump off a cliff or rope swing into the water but don't know where to go. Our book is for young folk looking for a good time and a place to chill. It's for older folk also looking for a good time and a place to chill, albeit with perhaps more modest swimwear.

This book is for anyone who likes to be in the water.

The Traditions of Living by Water

The lives of Pacific Northwest Native Americans—like the lives of all people—have revolved around water, as well as the animals within it, for millennia. Salmon is of great cultural and dietary importance, and if you grew up around here, there's a good chance you studied the incredible migrations of these iconic fish from rivers, lakes, and streams to the ocean and back again. Many of us who now live here can credit the arrival of European settlers, missionaries, and the logging industry; this change was a calamity for those whose ancestors had occupied the area for thousands of years. Today, Washington's twenty-nine federally recognized tribes (not all tribes are recognized) hold reservation land around these same rivers, Puget Sound, and the Pacific coast. The names of our towns, mountains, forests, and bodies of water are good cues to the long history of this region. Whether your ancestors crossed the Bering Strait twenty thousand years ago or you arrived on a plane last week, please keep in mind that we all share this land and the responsibility for its care. For more information on Washington tribes, check out the websites of the Duwamish Longhouse and Cultural Center and the Burke Museum of Natural History and Culture (see Resources).

WHAT MAKES A GREAT SWIMMING HOLE?

Because the great state of Washington has so much water, this book could have had a hundred thousand entries, but ultimately we had to limit ourselves. Siouxon Creek, Racehorse Creek Falls, the Mazama swimming hole on the Methow River, and Mountain Lake on Orcas Island are a few of our favorites—but there are so many others in this book that we love.

We took a few years to investigate swimming holes both near—close to our homes in Seattle, like Denny Blaine Beach—and far, like Colchuck Lake in the Enchantments and Palouse Falls south of Spokane. We went for dips in lakes and rivers and oceans, way up in the mountains or just a short bus ride from downtown Seattle. We even hunted north and

The incredible geology of the Lewis River (Swim #10)

south, in Oregon and British Columbia, as well as east and west, in Florida and Hawaii, just for the comparison. We dedicated a considerable amount of time to the water, looking for the important information:

> Who tends to go there? Are they locals, outdoor recreationists, families, frat boys?
> What is it like? Secluded or crowded? Beachy or rocky? Icy cold, very cold, cold, or cool?
> Where is it located? Forest? Roadside? Cliff? Beach?
> When is the best time to go? This is almost always late May through October, though there are exceptions based on water flows, and year-round polar plunges are an option.
> Why should you go there? To swim, of course, but what else is there to do? Stand-up paddle? Jump off cliffs? Picnic? Camp?
> How do you get there? Mostly by car and/or on foot, though some places are also accessible by bike or bus, and one is by boat.

We also researched how to visit these places without getting yourself injured or killed or pissing anyone off: safety, etiquette, gear, and more.

We used all this information to determine what makes a swimming hole good, which to us means the cleanliness of the water, the beauty of the surrounding area, the company you'll find there (or wonderful lack thereof), what it takes to get to that particular spot, and what you can do once you're there. That said, Shane tends to prefer a river over a lake, while Anna likes lakes better than rivers.

Other than that difference, we agree on just about everything: We want a swimming hole to be big enough to swim in—we want to be able to take actual swim strokes. Ideally, it's deep enough to jump into and has rocks or cliffs from which to safely jump off. A little current is a fun river bonus, as it gives you something to play in—you can swim against the current or let it sweep you downstream, then swim back up the eddy and round and round again. Shane loves a rope swing.

Of course, clean and clear water is important—all the swimming holes listed are clean, but in terms of clearness some of them, like Lake Washington, have milfoil or other plant matter. And—not that there's any choice in the matter in the PNW—we like it to be cold enough so that it makes you feel alive, followed by the urge to lie out on a rock in the sun like a sleepy cat. Hot springs are not included in this book, and few of the swimming holes deserve the designation of "warm." Most are within a range of coldness from very cold to cold to cool to warm, based on our subjective interpretation. A good view, whether it's a wall of old-growth evergreen or a sweeping mountainside, is favorable. We prefer solitude but respect those who like a scene.

Now, let's pause here for a second. With any new guidebook, there's the possibility of upsetting people who reasonably fear that the book will give away all their secrets and inevitably ruin everything. This was not our intent, and we quickly discovered that, on the whole, this shouldn't be an issue: most of the places we visited are not secret. With a few exceptions, most of these swimming holes are known to some degree. That said, if you're new to a spot, no matter how famous or closely guarded it is, please recognize that locals may be enjoying that spot regularly, so respect not just the natural environment but the people, too. Pay attention to local custom, and behave appropriately!

Please also use this book wisely, with the awareness that water is as dangerous as it is essential. As it says on a sign at Lower Lewis Falls, "Beneath the beauty of flowing water lurks injury and death." Check out the next section, Swimming-Hole Etiquette and Safety.

This book is really just a jumping-off point (pun intended), and for every beautiful swimming hole we included there are a hundred equally gorgeous ones that we had to leave out. We hope that *Swimming Holes of Washington* will get you outside into one of the most beautiful places on Earth and inspire you to go out on your own in pursuit of the Most Epic Swimming Hole.

Pay attention to posted warnings. (Swim #30)

SWIMMING-HOLE ETIQUETTE AND SAFETY

A few tips about swimming-hole etiquette are in order, so that everyone can have an optimal experience out in the water. Following this is a section about safety considerations so that you not only have fun but come home safe and sound too.

> Don't keep valuables in your car. Bring what you need for the hike or the stay, and leave the rest at home. Visible items attract burglars—not only to your car, but to everyone's vehicle in the parking area.

> Obey the backcountry camping rule: Leave the site better than you found it. Pack up your trash and take it with you when you leave. (See information on Leave No Trace at the back of this book.)

> Don't bug anglers. Fortunately, fisherfolk tend to be out on the water at the beginning and end of the day, whereas swimmers like the middle of the day for optimal warmth and sun. If you do get in the water while anglers are out there too, stay away from them, since your splashing and swimming will chase the fish away.

> Obey land-use regulations such as permits, closures, leash rules for dogs, etc. They're there for a reason.

> Respect wildlife.

> Respect the natural environment.

> Respect the people, too.

Look before you leap. Better yet, check the depth and understand the risks of jumping into rivers and lakes (Swim #1).

Rules of the Holes

The following rules are essential to having a safe and happy swim experience:

› Check the water conditions before you get in. When in doubt, stay out.
› No glass. Bare feet will thank you.
› Alcohol and drugs and swimming don't mix. Duh.
› Rope swings are dangerous. If you didn't put the rope in the tree, you are trusting that whoever did knew what they were doing. Always check the condition of the rope, the knots, and the tree.
› Confirm the water's depth before you jump, swing, or dive. And even then, remember that jumping and diving into water is dangerous.
› Cliff jumping is dangerous. There are all kinds of ways to slip, tumble, and fall. Be aware of your surroundings.
› Life is dangerous. So be careful. And have fun!

Flipping excited to be swimming on
Orcas Island (Swim #53)

HOW TO USE THIS GUIDE

AS WE MENTIONED IN the Introduction, there are thousands of potential swimming holes in Washington State, popular or undiscovered or visited by only those in the know. We cover a selection of swim spots across the state, from the Olympic Peninsula in the west to Palouse Falls State Park in the east, from the Columbia Gorge in the south to North Cascades National Park in the north. We include many spots where all you have to do is pull off the highway, others that require a short walk from the road, and some where you'll need to make a hike of it.

The swims are in twelve chapters arranged from south to north, starting at the Columbia Gorge (with a couple of spots on the Oregon side) and working up to the Bellingham area and north. Within this south-to-north geographical organization, we start from the west and work toward the east, including all the swimming holes along each corridor—such as Interstate 90 over Snoqualmie Pass, US Highway 2 over Stevens Pass, and State Route 20 through the North Cascades to the Methow Valley. Every chapter has a brief overview of that area, describing its major bodies of water.

For each swimming hole, we begin with a list of key facts, described below, followed by driving directions to the parking spot and a description that provides history, highlights, and insider's tips, all set up to make the book easy to use. Some swims include a map, but those with easy roadside access don't. Photos of the scenery give an idea of what to expect. Here's what the list of key facts includes:

TYPE: This listing describes what the body of water is, from a lake to a creek or river to saltwater, as well as its relative elevation with terms such as *lowland* for sea level up to about 2000 feet, *mountain forest* for 2000 to about 4000 feet, *subalpine* for 4000 feet to about 6000 or 7000 feet, or *alpine* for 6000 or 7000 feet or higher. In addition, this entry mentions if the spot has a water feature such as a waterfall, pool, eddy, or current, as well as a land feature such as a cliff jump or (sandy) beach.

LOCATION: Here you'll find details including proximity of the swim spot to parking, whether roadside (500 feet or less), a short walk (0.1 mile to 0.25 mile), or a hike-in (anything longer than 0.25 mile), so you can gauge how far in you want to haul your cooler and water toys; one swim is boat-in only. Other specifics include any protected designation, such as park (city, state, or national), national forest, or wilderness area, as well as the closest town and highway access.

WATER: This listing describes the temperature, clarity (visibility), and color of the swimming hole's water. Water temperature is subjective, with designations ranging from very cold to cold to cool to warm based on our experiences. Visibility and cleanliness can be anywhere from crystal clear to a little bit murky to opaque, depending on glacial silt, plant matter, etc. In general, this information indicates how far you can see through the water—from not at all to all the way to the bottom of a 20-foot-deep pool. Most water in this book is blue, but some swimming holes have other amazing colors that are described in this listing. Keep in mind, though, that water is clear, and in nature water is not just one color. At any given swimming hole, a multitude of colors come to mind whether you are under-water or backlit or staring into the sun or if it's a cloudy day, but if you scoop up a glass of the water it would be clear, so our descriptions of the color of the water are subjective.

SEASON: For the most part, this listing provides a standard range for swimming in the Pacific Northwest: spring or late spring through summer and fall, or roughly late May through October. Note that when we say summer, we literally mean June 21 (on average) through September 21. Of course some years, Mother Nature will let you in earlier, and

Dog days of summer on the Snoqualmie River (Swim #28)

some years, you'll have to be patient. Some places are potentially OK year round, depending on your cold-water and cold-weather tolerance. The swimming season for rivers depends on a safe water level as well as low flow for safe currents. In a couple of locations, seasonal closures are mentioned too.

WHO'S HERE: This is where we tell you every swimming hole that is kid-friendly and/or dog-friendly. (Keep in mind that even if an area is dog-friendly, that doesn't necessarily mean that Bowser can run around freely. Dogs must be leashed at all state parks, and even the most dog-loving strangers probably don't like having a strange dog shake all over them.) Other information ranges from whether there are crowds or not to what kind of folks are there, from hipsters to locals, teens to tourists, outdoor recreationists to RVers. We also mention some edgy possibilities such as nudity, drinking, and pot smoking so you can choose the places that suit you.

AMENITIES: This listing gives the basics, from parking to restrooms with flush toilets and running water (and showers if available) versus outhouses, plus drinking water, garbage cans, and/or shelter. Other features might include a rope swing, a dock, picnic tables, grills, fire rings, and camping, which could be anything from an isolated camp spot for DIY camping to backcountry camping to designated campgrounds. This entry also lists activities such as fishing, boating, playgrounds, volleyball courts, visitor centers, ranger stations, wheelchair-accessible facilities, and food available onsite, including ice-cream stands and campground stores. We also mention if places to go for camping, food, or lodging are nearby.

NOTES: Here we share what we know about any significant access issues such as road conditions, including if good clearance and/or four-wheel drive is necessary; whether a permit, pass, or entry fee is required; and dog-leash rules, if any. Not all places that require a pass have a way to buy them onsite so plan ahead and obtain any necessary passes in advance (see Resources).

LOCAL'S TIP: For every swimming hole, we give you a great piece of local lore that will help make your visit memorable.

GPS COORDINATES: This entry provides the north latitude and west longitude for the parking spot for each swimming hole, which may be more useful than the name of the swimming hole if you are using navigation devices. We've also listed GPS coordinates for the swimming hole itself in those cases where it seemed like they would be helpful.

GETTING THERE: Following the key facts described above, we provide driving directions and mileages from the nearest major highway and/or town to the parking area for the swim. Sometimes this parking spot is just a roadside pullout; for other swims you park in a developed campground or at a trailhead. From the parking spot, most swims are a short walk of a few hundred yards up to a quarter mile. If a hike of more than a quarter mile is required to get to the swimming hole, this paragraph gives basic information on the one-way distance and elevation gain (if any), as well as the high point on the hike in—but details about the hike itself are in the description of the swim. Subheadings and details are included in Getting There if other means of transportation to the hole are also possible, such as city bus or bicycle, or required, such as boating in.

It goes without saying that you should double-check directions before you go. Roads are constantly in flux—for example, washed out by floods, buried in snow or by an avalanche, or turned into superhighways. If a hike is required, check trail conditions too.

After all the nuts and bolts, we dive into the reasons we're all here: how to reach the hole once you've left your wheels behind and what you can do once you're at the water. We share our perspective about the place, the people there, what it's like to swim there, and what kind of water gear you should bring.

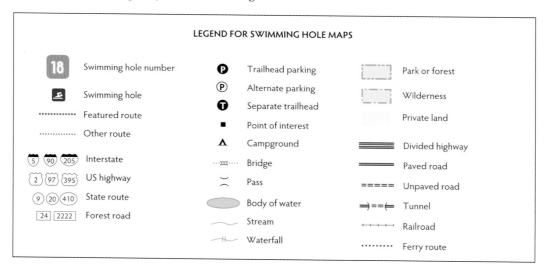

FIRE AND FLOOD

One of the things that makes the natural world so intriguing is that it is constantly changing. During our time exploring Washington State while researching and writing this book, we experienced one of the driest summers on record and several historic fire cycles. Rivers flood, forests burn, and nature grows back, one sapling at a time. The conditions represented in this book are a snapshot in time, and will most definitely change. Most notably, the Eagle Creek Fire of 2017 affected the Columbia River Gorge and the second swimming hole in this book, Punchbowl Falls on Eagle Creek. At the time this book went to press the area was closed, but we're hopeful it will be reopened in the future so we've left the description in place. Particularly for this swimming hole, but really for all locations in this book, be sure to check current conditions before heading out. And remember that you don't want to be the one to put an area out of commission; be careful out there!

Bring an underwater camera and take your selfies to a whole new level.

RECOMMENDED GEAR

This list includes gear that will make your swimming-hole visit easier—for example, water shoes make navigating a pebbly shore easier—and therefore potentially more enjoyable and more conducive to fun (also see The 10 Essentials sidebar):

> Swimsuit
> Towel
> Sunscreen
> Sunglasses
> Water shoes
> Sun shirts, hats, etc.
> Warm layers if appropriate
> Drinking water or water-purification system, if necessary
> Picnic supplies

OPTIONAL GEAR

Less is more, true, but sometimes it's fun to carry water toys—Frisbees! Inner tubes!—along with the basics. Here are some items to consider:

> › Goggles
> › Floaties (inflatables) such as noodles, armbands, lounges, etc.
> › Frisbee
> › Sun tent or umbrella
> › Stand-up paddleboard (SUP)
> › Inner tube
> › Fishing pole
> › Underwater camera
> › Hiking gear for a hike-in swim
> › Car-camping gear for an overnight near a parking spot
> › Backcountry camping gear for an overnight to a hike-in swim

The 10 Essentials

The point of the 10 Essentials, originated by The Mountaineers, has always been to answer two basic questions: Can you prevent emergencies and respond positively should one occur (items 1–5)? And can you safely spend a night—or more—outside (items 6–10)? Use this list as a guide and tailor it to the needs of your outing.

1. Navigation
2. Headlamp
3. Sun protection
4. First aid
5. Knife
6. Fire
7. Shelter
8. Extra food
9. Extra water
10. Extra clothes

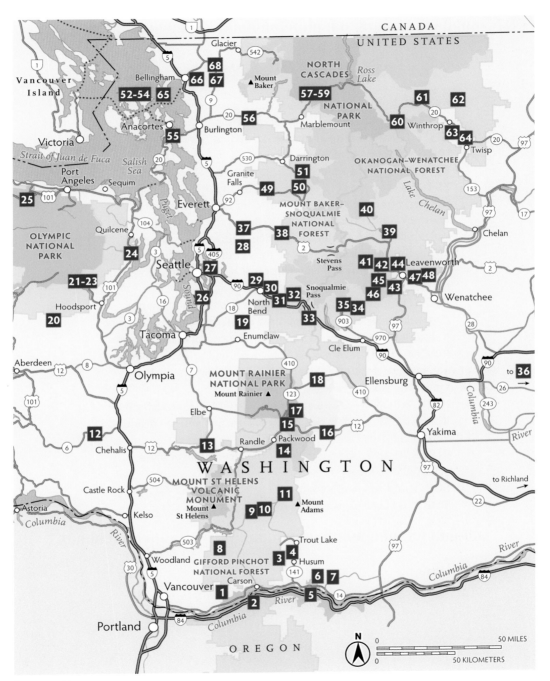

Overview Map

Important Words to Know

BEACH: sand or dirt shoreline that's easy on bare feet; we don't call pebbly, gravelly, or rocky shores "beaches"

CLIFF JUMP: a jump of more than 10 feet, whether from a bluff, cliff, rock, bridge, etc.

DIVE: a jump of 10 feet or less from rocks, logs, etc.

EDDY: a calm spot or area where the current is moving upriver, often located behind a rock or at a bend in the river; an eddy is usually on the inside of the bend, though it can sometimes form on the outside. Eddies make for great swimming because not only do they create a low-current zone, they also encourage the deposition of sediment, which collects to form a sand beach.

FLOATIE: personal flotation devices such as body boards and inflatables like tubes, lounges, small floats in the shape of unicorns or flamingos, armbands and vests, pool noodles, etc.

POCKET: small swimming hole on a small creek; colloquial and general term often used by locals to describe locally known swimming holes

PUNCHBOWL: deep swimming hole with a roundish shape

RIVER LEFT: the left side of the river when you are oriented downriver

RIVER RIGHT: the right side of the river when you are oriented downriver

SUP: stand-up paddleboard

TUBING: floating on an inner tube

Mirror Lake (Swim #33)

A NOTE ABOUT SAFETY

Safety is an important concern in all outdoor activities. No guidebook can alert you to every hazard or anticipate the limitations of every reader. Therefore, the descriptions of rivers, lakes, pools, roads, trails, and other features in this book are not representations that a particular place or excursion will be safe for your party. When you visit any of the swimming holes described in this book, you assume responsibility for your own safety. Under normal conditions, such excursions require the usual attention to traffic, road and trail conditions, weather, terrain, water conditions, the capabilities of your party, and other factors. Because many of the lands in this book are subject to development and/or change of ownership, conditions may have changed since this book was written that make your use of some of these locations unwise. Always check for current conditions, obey posted private-property signs, and avoid confrontations with property owners or managers. Keeping informed on current conditions and exercising common sense are the keys to a safe, enjoyable outing.

—Mountaineers Books

Summer feels right in Oregon at Punchbowl Falls. (Swim #2)

COLUMBIA RIVER GORGE

THE COLUMBIA RIVER, the seventh-largest river in the United States, forms a natural border between Washington and Oregon. The 75-mile-long section known as the Columbia River Gorge is the largest designated national scenic area in the United States. In this region, there's just about every outdoor activity imaginable, plus wine-tasting, shopping, dining, and museum touring in nearby communities. Interstate 84 on the Oregon side provides faster travel than State Route 14 on the Washington side, with bridges connecting Vancouver and Portland, White Salmon and Hood River, and Dallesport and North Dalles with The Dalles. Rivers on both sides of the gorge provide swimming holes: in addition to the Washougal, White Salmon, and Klickitat in Washington, we've included a couple of choice places on the Oregon side.

The Klickitat River, a 75-mile-long tributary of the Columbia River, is one of the bigger rivers in this book. What you might not realize as you drive to the town of Lyle, on SR 14 just south of where the Klickitat and the Columbia converge, is that the Klickitat is on the east side of the Cascade crest. The Klickitat's main glacial drainage arrives from the east side of Mount Adams, about 50 miles to the north, while the White Salmon's origins are on the west slopes of Mount Adams.

 ## WASHOUGAL RIVER: DOUGAN FALLS

TYPE: Lowland-forest river and creek, enough current to feel it, waterfall, pools, cliff jump
LOCATION: Roadside or short walk northeast of Washougal via SR 14 and Washougal River Road
WATER: Cool to warm, clear, blue-green

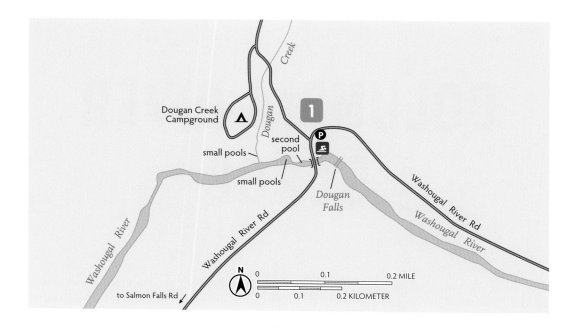

SEASON: Summer through fall
WHO'S HERE: Kid-friendly, dog-friendly; teens, barbecuers, nine-to-fivers, ne'er-do-wells
AMENITIES: Some parking; camping nearby
NOTES: Good roads with a bit of dirt road right at the end, but no problem for any car; day-use fee or Discover Pass required
LOCAL'S TIP: Don't go during peak midday hours.
GPS COORDINATES: 45.6727 N, −122.1533 W

GETTING THERE

From I-5 in Vancouver, take exit 1A to merge onto State Route 14 east toward Stevenson. (From Portland, head east to I-205 north and exit onto SR 14 east about 6 miles east of Vancouver.) After 26 miles, past the towns of Camas and Washougal and just past Cape Horn, turn left onto Salmon Falls Road. After 3.4 miles, turn right onto Washougal River Road. After 5.7 miles, cross the Washougal River and find a parking lot on your right.

This is the quintessential swimming hole, amazing and popular. All in all, this is what swimming holes are all about—lots of options: lots of deep, swimmable pools; lots of rocks to lounge on; lots of sun to soak up late in the day; and some cliff jumping. A great place to spend a day or most of the day, but you won't be alone.

From the parking lot, most folks head just upstream of the bridge to the main pool. It's a bit more treacherous to get up above the falls; downstream, you'll find smaller pools just past the bridge and also at the mouth of Dougan Creek. The cliffs here may look promising for cliff jumping but many of the pools aren't deep enough so don't try it; you don't want to win a Darwin Award. Instead hold off until you reach the main pool, which is is big and deep—in fact, it's so deep in the middle that you can't see the bottom. It's like a big swimming pool, with a gorgeous waterfall feeding into it. Bring your goggles and a noodle. There's a fair amount of space to hang out around this main pool, which makes it prime real estate for chilling.

Above the falls you can find some smaller pools and slides. These tend to be less crowded, likely because the terrain is a little more treacherous. It may not be the best place for children who are new to walking or other people who may be wobbly on their feet.

Just downstream of the main pool and the bridge is a really nice pool, still big enough to swim around in and deep enough to jump into in select areas. Be aware that there are submerged boulders here, so be sure to look before you leap. The boulders provide an obstacle course to swim around and climb onto to catch that golden late-afternoon sun—generally, there's better late-afternoon sun downstream of the bridge. From here, the river

Come early and then stay for the late-afternoon sun.

Mermaid sighting on the Washougal River

disperses into smaller pools, where you'll find a gentler current, suitable for kids with good swim skills and supervision, as well as more space away from the crowds.

Downstream on the right, the small tributary of Dougan Creek joins the Washougal, and it has its own little pools that are a bit colder and shadier. This makes a nice spot for kids to play in and explore the shallows and for all of humanity to find some shady refuge during the heat of the day.

One of the perks of Dougan Falls is that it catches the late-afternoon sun, so good times can roll beyond the usual peak hours of midday. If you've spent the day enjoying the numerous activities of the Columbia River Gorge, maybe biking, hiking, kite surfing, shopping, or golfing, Dougan Falls is an awesome way to wrap things up. However, this is a popular spot—and for good reason—so if you want to find a place to lay your towel, the earlier the better.

It's also close to Portland—roughly an hour away—so that if you're heading to or coming from there after work, there's still enough time to catch some rays and some swim time on long summer days. If you want to spend the night, Dougan Creek Campground is right near the falls, but it's small and doesn't take reservations so you'll have to get there early to claim a spot.

 ## EAGLE CREEK: PUNCHBOWL FALLS (OREGON)

TYPE: Lowland-forest creek, waterfall
LOCATION: Hike-in in Columbia Gorge National Scenic Area east of Bonneville, OR, via I-84
WATER: Cold, very clear, blue-green
SEASON: Summer, until the rains come
WHO'S HERE: PDX hipsters trying to get the most rad Instagram selfie, tourists, hikers, outdoor recreationists
AMENITIES: Outhouse
NOTES: Although the devastating 2017 Eagle Creek Fire started in Eagle Creek drainage, Punchbowl Falls appears to have suffered minimal damage as compared to the ridge tops and other areas of the Columbia River Gorge. The hike to the swimming hole is still through fire-affected areas, however, and the trail is closed at the time of publication. Check current conditions, and remember that our actions have consequences: *always* practice Leave No Trace techniques when using our natural resources. Northwest Forest Pass required.
LOCAL'S TIP: Grab some excellent food and drink at McMenamins in Troutdale.
GPS COORDINATES: 45.6383 N, −121.9203 W (trailhead); 45.6216 N, −121.8945 W (Punchbowl Falls)

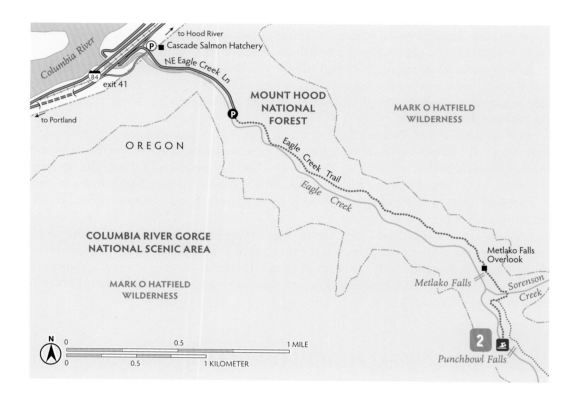

GETTING THERE

From Portland, take I-84 east to exit 41 (Eagle Creek, Fish Hatchery). Turn right, and in 0.1 mile where the road Ts at the Cascade Salmon Hatchery, bear right onto NE Eagle Creek Lane. Continue for 0.4 mile to Eagle Creek trailhead #440. If the lot is full, park back at the picnic area near the hatchery. Follow the Eagle Creek Trail about 2 miles (elevation gain: 500 feet; high point: 600 feet).

Along the Columbia River Gorge and just across the border in Oregon, cathedral-like Punchbowl Falls is so gorgeous it just might take your breath away. Whether you live nearby or you're just passing through, every person should visit Punchbowl Falls at least once for that true Pacific Northwest experience. The water is cold, in large part because Punchbowl Falls is essentially in a deep gorge and therefore protected from the sun. It's surrounded by moss-covered rock walls, so the sun can shine in for only a slice of the day, and of course this is when the area draws the most crowds. If you're willing to brave some shade, come at off-peak times for more wiggle room.

From the Eagle Creek trailhead, Punchbowl Falls is an easy, approximately 2-mile hike. The trail varies from wide and well maintained along the creek to more overgrown in the lush deciduous rain forest and along narrow cliff edges with sprawling valley views. People often use the terms "fairyland" and "hobbit landscape" or "straight out of *Lord of the Rings*" when describing this trail. Be aware that a couple spots have steep exposure, and with a lot of people sharing the trail, you will have to be careful at certain pinch points; for this reason, keep kids and dogs close if you choose to bring them to this spot. You'll pass Metlako Falls Overlook at 1.5 miles, and after crossing Sorenson Creek, 0.2 mile beyond the Overlook, head right on the Lower Punchbowl Falls Trail for a short way.

Most people come to take photos without getting in the water, so the biggest crowds will be at midday, walking along the cobble beach searching for photo ops. It is totally worth coming just for the sight-seeing—don't forget your waterproof camera. You can get away from the crowd by wading in the shallows, then swimming up to the superdeep

Cross the border into Oregon for some Punchbowl Falls time.

pool at the base of the waterfall and hanging out on the small cliff ledges around the punchbowl. Bring a drybag if you'd like to keep valuables with you.

Right where the trail drops down to river level, you'll see a smaller set of falls with a small pool at the base. This is where people like to cliff jump but, as always, check the water depth and the exit before jumping. There is often a rope set to climb out on, but beware the condition and safety of the rope, and scout out a way to hike around before you take the leap. Farther downstream is 100-foot Metlako Falls, so be mindful of the current.

If you want to hang out, consider packing a hoodie or fleece, and if you do get a little chilled, don't worry—you'll catch some sun on the hike back out and be plenty warmed up by the time you get to your car. To regain that refreshed feeling, hop back in the creek at the trailhead before heading home.

For more hiking, continue on the main Eagle Creek Trail up to High Bridge (3.3 miles from the trailhead), Tunnel Falls (6 miles from the trailhead), or Wahtum Lake (13.3 miles from the trailhead).

3 BUCK CREEK POCKET

TYPE: Lowland-forest creek, waterfall, pool
LOCATION: Roadside, with hike-in option to avoid creek crossing, north of White Salmon via SR 14 and SR 141
WATER: Cool, not crystal clear, shady dark green
SEASON: Summer and fall
WHO'S HERE: Locals, high schoolers, people in the know
AMENITIES: None at roadside pulloff; outhouse at trailhead
LOCAL'S TIP: Check out Camp 1805 Distillery across the Columbia in Hood River, OR, for locally made spirits and food.
GPS COORDINATES: 45.8172 N, −121.5430 W

GETTING THERE

From I-5 south of Woodland, take exit 7 onto I-205/Veterans Memorial Freeway south, toward NE 134th Street and Salem. You have two options: (1) Take exit 27 onto State Route 14 and continue eastbound for 57.8 miles toward the town of White Salmon. Just before town, turn left on SR 141. (2) For a faster drive (but requiring a small toll), stay on I-205 across the Columbia River into Oregon. After 14.8 miles, take exit 22 for I-84/US 30 east toward The Dalles. After 55.5 miles, take exit 64 for OR 35 toward Mount Hood Highway, White Salmon, and Government Camp. After 0.3 mile, turn left (north) onto OR 35/Button Bridge Road. After 0.1 mile, the road becomes Hood River Bridge across the Columbia back into Washington. After 1.1 miles, turn left (west) onto SR 14 in White Salmon. **FROM EITHER OPTION:** After 1.5 miles, turn right (north) onto SR 141 Alt, then bear left onto SR 141. Once you are on SR 141, go 4.1 miles and turn left onto Northwestern Lake Road/Forest Road 80. Go 0.5 mile, crossing the White Salmon River, and continue through an intersection with Lakeview Road, after which the road turns into Nester Peak Road (getting to this spot is the crux of finding this swimming hole). Go another 0.5 mile and take the right fork onto Buck Creek Road. Continue 2.6 miles to the Buck Creek trailhead, then hike 0.5 mile on the Buck Creek Trail (elevation gain: 75 feet; high point: 950 feet).

The Buck Creek Pocket is like a perfect little footnote to Swim #5, Mosier Creek Pocket, and Swim #4, White Salmon River: Below Husum Falls. Driving up to Buck Creek, you might be skeptical that there would be anything worthwhile here. But sure enough, the little creek pours through a teeny-tiny gorge and drops into a waterfall that cascades down into a pothole of a swim spot.

Tiny swimming hole, big fun

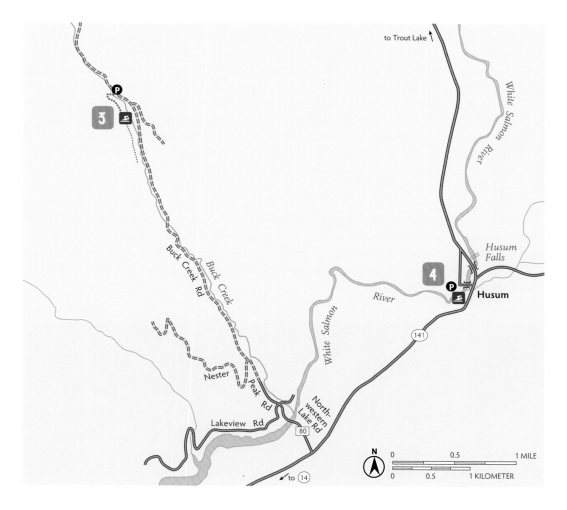

This swimming hole is very small, and any more than ten people would be a crowd, but it'd be rare to see that many people here. A fair amount of sun shines through to warm the water and the basalt shoreline, and even toward the end of summer it has a good amount of flow. Since it's a small drainage, it could dry out, but only in a really dry summer, and it probably doesn't get too high except in the peak of spring snowmelt and rainfall. Of course, be aware of the same dangers here as you would for any river.

It is a classic Northwest swim spot in the mossy, foresty kind of way, and for many, that is what makes it so novel and cool: it's up a back road, it's not heavily traveled, it's brushy and leafy and not crystal clear. And it can involve some acrobatics and bushwhacking, if you so choose. Instagrammers might just overlook this spot, but in-the-know locals will not, especially on summer's hottest days.

4 WHITE SALMON RIVER: BELOW HUSUM FALLS

TYPE: Lowland river, waterfall, pool
LOCATION: Roadside north of White Salmon via SR 14 and SR 141, across Columbia River Gorge from Hood River, OR
WATER: Very cold, clear, blue-green
SEASON: Mid- to late summer
WHO'S HERE: Rafters, kayakers, mountain bikers, climbers, hikers
AMENITIES: Food nearby
LOCAL'S TIP: Wet Planet Rafting and Kayaking is immediately across the road; in addition to offering rafting and kayak rental, they sell coffee and snacks.
GPS COORDINATES: 45.79747 N, –121.48549 W

The glorious White Salmon River—just note the whitewater rapid downstream, and take care!

GETTING THERE

From I-5 south of Woodland, take exit 7 onto I-205/Veterans Memorial Freeway south, toward NE 134th Street and Salem. You have two options: (1) Take exit 27 onto State Route 14 eastbound for 57.8 miles toward the town of White Salmon, and just before town, turn left on SR 141. (2) For a faster drive (but requiring a small toll), stay on I-205 across the Columbia River into Oregon. After 14.8 miles, take exit 22 to merge onto I-84/US 30 east toward The Dalles. After 55.5 miles, take exit 64 for OR 35 toward Mount Hood Highway, White Salmon, and Government Camp. After 0.3 mile, turn left (north) onto OR 35/Button Bridge Road. After 0.1 mile, the road becomes Hood River Bridge across the Columbia back into Washington. After 1.1 miles, turn left (west) onto SR 14 in White Salmon. **FROM EITHER OPTION:** After 1.5 miles, turn right (north) onto SR 141 Alt, then bear left onto SR 141. Once you are on SR 141, go north 6.1 miles past a couple of roads, and just before a bridge over the White Salmon River, look for parking on the left side of the highway across from Wet Planet Rafting and Kayaking.

The White Salmon River is renowned for its whitewater kayaking and rafting; it and the Little Salmon River are some of the most popular rivers for recreation in Washington State. People have been known to climb Mount Adams, ski down from the summit, mountain bike to the White Salmon River, and then paddle to the Columbia Gorge. The area from Mount Adams to the Gorge is highly recommended for outdoor athletes of all stripes. This is a roadside swim spot—State Route 141 parallels the White Salmon River as you drive upriver from town and the Columbia River Gorge.

Husum Falls isn't all that big as far as waterfalls go, maybe 10 or 15 feet tall, but don't let its size fool you—it is very dangerous during higher water flows and not worth swimming underneath at those times because of that. High-water season is usually spring into early summer, with July 4th generally being a reliable marker for the start of the swimming season here. If the previous winter saw a big snowpack, however, the water may be too high for safe and enjoyable swimming until later in the summer. Check that water isn't too high or flowing too fast, to avoid whitewater rapids downstream at high flows.

From your parking spot, it's just a few steps down to the water. The swimming hole is just downstream of the falls, under Husum Street Bridge over the river. Whitewater rafters often portage at the waterfall and stop here for some bridge or rock jumping. You'll notice that these folks usually have life jackets on. This swimming hole becomes more popular as the weather gets hotter and the water levels lower.

The pool is a deep, gorged-out channel of the river, both glacial- and spring-fed. No matter how prepared you are, the cold will take your breath away, even at the end of the season. There's not much beach or shoreline, so there's no good picnic or lounge zone. Stop here for some fun times jumping in and cooling off rather than to hang out after kayaking, rafting, trail running, mountain biking, or hiking.

MOSIER CREEK POCKET (OREGON)

TYPE: Lowland creek, waterfall, cliff jump
LOCATION: Hike-in near Mosier, OR, via I-84/US 30
WATER: Cool to warm, clearish, cleanish, blue-green
SEASON: Spring and summer; might dry up in the fall
WHO'S HERE: Locals, PDX hipsters, Gorge enthusiasts
AMENITIES: None; everything you need is nearby in town
LOCAL'S TIP: If you happen to be in the tiny town of Mosier (population less than 500) on the second Sunday of the month, bring your ukelele and join the Uke Group at the Mosier Grange.
GPS COORDINATES: 45.6840 N, –121.3977 W (trailhead); 45.6825 N, –121.3903 W (swimming hole)

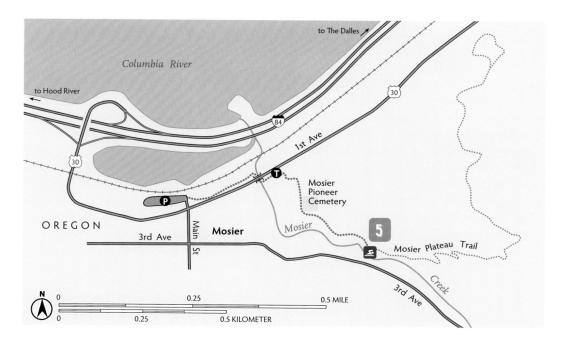

Mosier Pocket—an oasis on the southeast side of the Columbia River Gorge

From I-84 east, take exit 69 to Mosier via US Highway 30, which turns into First Avenue. At the stop sign at Main Street, turn left (north) and park on the left side of the road (look for the Mosier totem pole). Walk east along First Avenue, cross the bridge over Mosier Creek, and reach the Mosier Plateau trailhead. Hike about 0.75 mile on the Mosier Plateau Trail (elevation gain: 100 feet; high point: 225 feet).

Despite being so close to where Mosier Creek flows into the Columbia River, at first glance the Mosier Pocket looks like a trickle, with hardly enough water to bother. Some years, it probably does dry up all the way. Since this area is east of the Cascades, it is hotter and drier than the west side. On the flip side, that means that the water level is low enough to swim in earlier in the season, and the sunshine is hot more often than not. This makes the Mosier Pocket feel like an unexpected oasis next to the sun-scorched hillside.

From the parking lot in the town of Mosier, the route to the swimming hole takes roughly ten or fifteen minutes, unless you get distracted by the Mosier Pioneer Cemetery (established in 1865) just a couple minutes into the hike. Originally the family cemetery of the Mosiers, this historical burial ground contains the moss-covered headstones of the friends and relatives of the city's founders, the last of whom was laid to rest here in 1901. The hike is the perfect length to get you good and hot so that you'll be looking forward to a refreshing dip when you get to the pools.

As you approach the main swimming hole, you'll actually first come to a cliff-jump spot. Mosier Creek is not the clearest creek in the Gorge, so if you choose to jump—which is always dangerous—please thoroughly check your landing first. If you're not jumping, climb down into the swimming hole—taking care because, as you'll notice, you'll be above a large cascading waterfall. Both the jump and the waterfall make this spot too dangerous for younger children to visit.

Start your hike back still dripping wet—by the time you get back to your car, the hot eastern Cascades breeze will have dried you off. For a longer and therefore more heat-producing hike, when you get to the swim spot keep going on the Mosier Plateau Trail for the 3.5-mile round-trip, and stop for a swim on your way back.

6 KLICKITAT RIVER: AT LYLE

TYPE: Lowland river, cliff jump
LOCATION: Short walk in Lyle via SR 14
WATER: Cold to cool, slightly milky, cleanish, greenish
SEASON: Late spring through early fall

The big rope swing under the bridge in Lyle

WHO'S HERE: Adventurers, those with courage
AMENITIES: Parking, rope swing; park, restrooms in park; food nearby (in Lyle and across the Columbia in Hood River, OR)
LOCAL'S TIP: Go 4 miles up the Columbia (to mile marker 183) to Dougs Beach for some epic windsurfing.
GPS COORDINATES: 45.6973 N, –121.2921 W

GETTING THERE

From I-5 south of Woodland, take exit 7 onto I-205/Veterans Memorial Freeway south toward NE 134th Street and Salem. You have two options: (1) Take exit 27 onto State Route 14 eastbound for 70.6 miles to Lyle. (2) For a faster drive, which requires a small toll, stay on I-205 across the Columbia River into Oregon. After 14.8 miles, take exit 22 to merge onto I-84/US Highway 30 east toward The Dalles. After 55.5 miles, take exit 64 for OR 35 toward Mount Hood Highway, White Salmon, and Government Camp. After 0.3 mile, turn left (north) onto OR 35/Button Bridge Road. After 0.1 mile, the road becomes Hood River Bridge across the Columbia back into Washington. (From Portland it's about 64 miles to the Hood River Bridge via US 30 east and I-84 east.) After 1.1 miles, turn right (east) onto SR 14. After 10.7 miles, arrive at the Lyle bridge.

The town of Lyle was originally known as Klickitat Landing, part of a trading route used by the Indian tribes of the region. (In 1876, a settler renamed the town after himself.) Underneath the State Route 14 bridge, right in the center of town, a giant rope swing beckons, as well as cliffs itching to be jumped off into the Klickitat River flowing by with little current, here at the river's mouth. Due to its lack of beaches, this spot is for the adventurer type and those happy to offer moral support.

The cliff jump and rope swing are on river right, a short walk down from the parking area. On river left a community park has a paved parking area, nice public restrooms, and the Klickitat trailhead. You can park on either side of the bridge; from the park it's about a 0.1-mile walk across the bridge to the rope-swing side.

The rope swing is decidedly not for the meek—though you grab the rope from shore, it's attached to the bridge itself, and you will have 15–20 feet of air time before splashdown. Before cliff jumping or rope swinging, scout your exit from the water since it's a mostly cliff-lined shore (though it's likely you'll meet folks down there who can point you in the right direction).

 ## 7 KLICKITAT RIVER: THREE MILE

TYPE: Lowland river, very strong current in spring, eddies, beach
LOCATION: Roadside northeast of Lyle via SR 14 and SR 142
WATER: Cold to cool, clear, blue-green
SEASON: Mid- to late summer
WHO'S HERE: Locals, recreationists
AMENITIES: Food nearby in Lyle
LOCAL'S TIP: If you're in the mood for a hike, walk the nearly level 31-mile rail corridor along the Klickitat River from Lyle to the Goldendale Plateau.
GPS COORDINATES: 45.7221 N, –121.2474 W

GETTING THERE

From I-5 south of Woodland, take exit 7 onto I-205/Veterans Memorial Freeway south toward NE 134th Street and Salem. You have two options: (1) Take exit 27 onto State Route 14 eastbound for 70.6 miles to Lyle. (2) For a faster drive, which requires a small toll, stay on I-205 across the Columbia River into Oregon. After 14.8 miles, take exit 22 to merge onto I-84/US Highway 30 east toward The Dalles. After 55.5 miles, take exit 64 for OR 35 toward Mount Hood Highway, White Salmon, and Government Camp. After 0.3 mile, turn left (north) onto OR 35/Button Bridge Road. After 0.1 mile, the road becomes Hood River Bridge across the Columbia back into Washington. (From Portland, it's about 64 miles to the Hood River Bridge via US 30 east and I-84 east.) After 1.1 miles, turn right (east) onto SR 14. After 10.8 miles, turn left onto SR 142. After 2.9 miles, pull off on the right side of the road and park.

Just one of the many great spots to swim along the Klickitat River

The Klickitat River is a favorite among rafters and anglers and other outdoorsfolks (think hunters and anglers more than hikers). The entire Klickitat River is good for swimming, with lots of access points from State Route 142, which parallels the river for many miles. The region is warmer, drier, and a little more deserty than the western Washington environment, with potential for poison ivy to be growing nearby.

At low volume, much of the river is calm with lots of big eddies. However, there are two exceptions to the generally placid nature of the Klickitat, which is good news for the many whitewater rafters who come to the Klickitat specifically for some adventure.

The first caveat is that, about 1 mile upstream from Lyle and the Columbia River, a Class V whitewater section is created by the river squeezing through a very narrow gorge. Even if the water is low, the narrowness of this gorge makes for very strong and dangerous currents. It is likely people still swim here, but this is not the section we recommend; instead, drive 3 miles upriver from Lyle.

The second caveat is that in the spring, when the river level is up, the current is very strong even at Three Mile. Every year there are accidents on this river because people try to swim or tube when the current is too strong. To avoid this pitfall, wait until later in the summer.

From the roadside pullout, it's a short walk (100 feet) along the obvious trail to the water. Watch out for poison ivy along this trail, and make sure dogs and kids stay close. You'll be in the clear once you get to the river.

This area has wonderful eddies, and even at low water, there's enough current to swim against and play in. Bring your inner tube. Three Mile has a small sandy beach with some rocks to lounge on. There are lots of access points along the river, so if this exact location doesn't appeal, find another spot!

Even when the water is low, there is a consistent current along the Klickitat River.

"Paradise Found" on Siouxon Creek
(Swim #8)

SOUTH CASCADES

MOST OF THE SOUTH CASCADES are located within national forest, specifically Gifford Pinchot National Forest, as well as the Columbia River Gorge National Scenic Area and Mount St. Helens National Volcanic Monument. This region extends from the northern shores of the Columbia River to Mount St. Helens and the Mount Adams Wilderness to the north. This is Bigfoot territory—and the locals won't let you forget it.

The Lewis River, one of this region's largest, is reached by State Route 503—which runs on both sides of the river: the SR 503 to Siouxon Creek is south of the river, and SR 503 to the Lewis River Falls is north of the river. The Lewis River is big, so it has fluctuations in water flow. The falls have big pools below them, which make for great swimming, just keep in mind that at times the current is too strong to be safe. Ideally, wait for low water volume in the late summer, and just be careful if there is any current. Obviously, be cautious anytime you are near or above the falls. And remember, the water is extra cold in the spring and early summer!

 ## SIOUXON CREEK

TYPE: Lowland-forest creek, waterfalls, pools
LOCATION: Hike-in in Gifford Pinchot National Forest east of Woodland and Amboy via I-5 and SR 503
WATER: Cold, very clear, very clean, emerald green
SEASON: Summer and early fall
WHO'S HERE: Hikers, backpackers, mountain bikers
AMENITIES: Parking, backcountry camping
NOTES: Potholed road, but most two-wheel-drive vehicles with moderate clearance should be fine; Northwest Forest Pass required
LOCAL'S TIP: Bring your night-vision goggles for Bigfoot sighting.
GPS COORDINATES: 45.9466 N, −122.1772 W

GETTING THERE

From I-5 at Woodland, take exit 21 toward Woodland and Cougar. Keep straight onto Pacific Avenue, which becomes Goerig Street. Turn left onto Lakeshore Drive, then take an immediate left onto State Route 503/Lewis River Road. After 0.1 mile, turn right onto East CC Street, which becomes NW Hayes Road/NW Pacific Highway. Keep left to stay on NW Hayes Road, which, after 4.1 miles, becomes NE Hayes Road. After 1.2 miles the name changes again to NE Cedar Creek Road. After 10.8 miles, turn right onto 221st Avenue in Amboy. After 0.2 mile, turn left onto SR 503. After 3.9 miles, turn right on NE Healy Road, then turn left to stay on NE Healy Road, followed by a right. After 2.3 miles the road name changes to Forest Road 54. After 6.9 miles, bear left onto unpaved Calamity Peak Road/FR 57. After 1.2 miles turn left on FR 5701. After 3.7 miles, park at the trailhead (space for roughly twenty cars) or roadside. Follow Siouxon Trail for up to 2.6 miles (200 feet elevation loss or up to 400 feet elevation gain depending on how far you go; high point: 1500 feet).

One of the luscious pools along Siouxon Creek

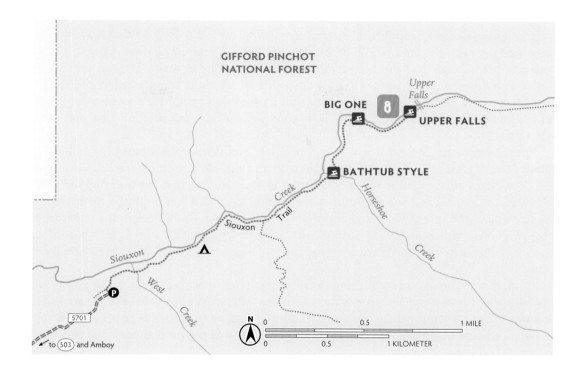

Not only might this be our favorite surprise discovery of the whole book, it's one of the top contenders for our favorite hike-in swim spots of all time—Siouxon Creek has amazing water quality and color. Located in Bigfoot and gnome country—Skamania County, to be precise—it requires a decent amount of time on Forest Service roads, so it takes longer to get to the trailhead than expected if you calculate travel time based on mileage. Because the hike to the first prime swimming hole is a couple of miles, plan on dedicating at least the better part of a day, or if you can spare it, devote a weekend: there are backcountry campsites on the trail about 0.6 mile from the trailhead. This spot is closer to Portland, so you can play the game "Portlander or Seattleite?" of guessing where other hikers are from. The difference is subtle, and this activity can provide entertainment for local folks chaperoning out-of-town relatives.

The road is good, with occasional potholes and bumps along the way. A vehicle with clearance wouldn't hurt, but it's not totally necessary, and two-wheel drive will be fine. Check with the Mount Adams ranger station to find the most current road conditions, and if you have friends with four-wheel drive, convince them to let you into their carpool. Since this is the Pacific Northwest, you'll likely find a lot of Subarus and Subaru-type cars.

You'll have driven through some heavily logged terrain, but don't let that scare you—once you get onto the trail, you'll be in classic PNW vegetation heaven. As is the case for most hikes, weekdays on the trail are less crowded. The Siouxon Trail crosses West Creek and drops about 200 feet to the campsites at 0.6 mile, then parallels the creek. In just over 0.5 mile farther, you reach a trail junction and the first decent swim spot, which has deep enough water to swim in and easy access—but this is just a tease for what's to come.

Keep going—the farther in you hike, the better and deeper the swimming holes. At about 1.8 miles and 100 feet of elevation gain from the trail's low point, you cross Horseshoe Creek, with an amazing little natural bathtub-like feature. The first big waterfall-fed pool is at about 2.2 miles and another 50 feet of elevation gain, and you might be surprised by its size and depth, given the character of Siouxon Creek up to this point. It's superdeep and gorgeous, with beautiful Siouxon Creek Falls pouring in. To access the swimming hole, you'll have to hike down a steep, eroding, and exposed hillside, so be careful on your way down.

If, after this one, your swimming-hole craving isn't totally satisfied, keep going for another 0.4 mile and 250 feet of elevation gain to a similar spot at the base of Upper Falls, 2.6 miles from the trailhead. This second waterfall has better rocks to jump off of, a log to balance-beam on, and smooth granite for easy access to the pool, though the previous waterfall is more photogenic.

If you go only this far, you'll have hit all the finest swimming holes the creek has to offer—and you'll have that last 200 feet of climbing to get back to your car at the end of the day. On the other hand, while the swimming holes you'll encounter if you keep going aren't as noteworthy, it's a beautiful hike and you could continue going upcreek for 2.5 miles. For you mountain bikers, there are many biking trails in the area (visit the MTB Project website for more information; see Resources at the back of the book). After your ride, you'll be all sweaty and dirty and ready to get in the water.

 ## LEWIS RIVER: LOWER FALLS

TYPE: Lowland-forest river, waterfall, pool, beach
LOCATION: Short walk in Gifford Pinchot National Forest northeast of Woodland and Cougar via I-5 and SR 503/FR 90
WATER: Cold, very clear, very clean, blue-green
SEASON: Summer through early fall
WHO'S HERE: Kid-friendly; weekend campers, RVers, PDX hipsters, photographers
AMENITIES: Parking, restrooms and composting toilets, drinking water, picnic tables, fire rings and grills, camping

Lewis River's Lower Falls are both photogenic and spectacular for swimming.

NOTE: Northwest Forest Pass required
LOCAL'S TIP: Bring the good camera.
GPS COORDINATES: 46.1568 N, –121.8785 W

GETTING THERE

From I-5 at Woodland, take exit 21 toward Woodland and Cougar and turn right onto Lewis River Road/State Route 503. Drive east on SR 503 through the town of Cougar. The road becomes Forest Road 90 at the Skamania County line. Continue east on FR 90 to a junction with FR 25, at about 47 miles from I-5. Turn right here to stay on FR 90. Cross the North Fork Lewis River and continue up FR 90 for about 14 miles to the Lower Falls Recreation Area. Turn right off FR 90, followed by another right into the Lower Lewis Falls Campground day-use parking area at Lower Lewis River Falls trailhead.

Close to Mount Adams and Mount St. Helens, Lewis River Lower Falls and Middle Falls (Swim #10) might be the best two swimming holes in Skamania County, if not the whole state. The waterfalls are absolutely stunning, with clear aquamarine glacial melt from Mount Adams. Lush old-growth forests in this area are rumored to harbor gnomes and, of course, the infamous Bigfoot. It's a very special place in Washington State, and to experience it more fully, stay at the Lower Falls Campground. As for all popular spots, go on a weekday to avoid the crowds.

From the Lewis River trailhead it is only a 500-foot walk to the Lower Falls vista, but to get to the actual pool, you have to traverse a steep unofficial trail 100 feet or so, which may be slippery at times.

The Lower Falls takes a 43-foot drop, and at its base a rock shelf surrounds the deep, stunning water. Big and wide, it's like a swimming pool, and at high water the rock shelf

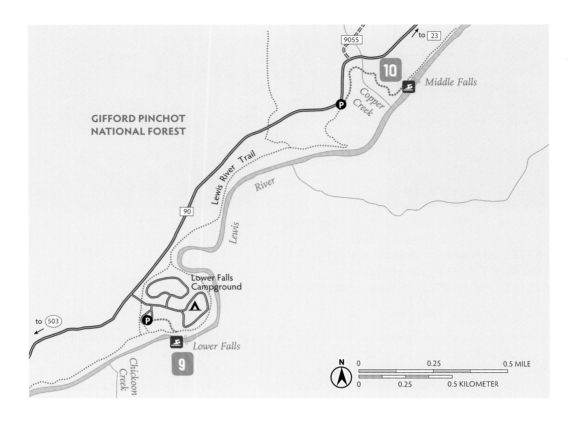

is not visible—the water cascades with aplomb from multiple channels. During low water, you can walk around in the shallow water on the shelf and dive from here into the deeper pool. The water itself is a deep turquoise blue, reflecting off the towering evergreens on all sides, which makes you feel like you're in a big tree enclave.

Upstream of Lower Falls, less than 0.25 mile along the Lewis River Trail, you can find a beach and some shallow water, which might be nice for kids. Of course, be aware that you are above a big waterfall.

 LEWIS RIVER: MIDDLE FALLS

TYPE: Lowland-forest river, waterfall
LOCATION: Hike-in in Gifford Pinchot National Forest northeast of Woodland and Cougar via I-5 and SR 503/FR90
WATER: Very cold, very clear, very clean, green

SEASON: Late summer
WHO'S HERE: Kid-friendly; weekend campers, RVers, PDX hipsters, photographers
AMENITIES: Parking, restrooms, picnic tables, fire rings; camping nearby
NOTE: Northwest Forest Pass required
LOCAL'S TIP: There are lots of underwater photo ops, too, so bring the underwater camera.
GPS COORDINATES: 46.1663 N, –121.8673 W (trailhead); 46.1670 N, –121.8632 W (swimming hole)

GETTING THERE

From I-5 at Woodland, take exit 21 toward Woodland and Cougar and turn right onto Lewis River Road/State Route 503. Drive east on SR 503 through the town of Cougar. The road becomes Forest Road 90 at the Skamania County line. Continue east on FR 90 to a junction with FR 25, at about 47 miles from I-5. Turn right here to stay on FR 90. Cross the North Fork Lewis River and continue up FR 90 to about 14 miles from FR 25, where you pass the Lower Falls Recreation Area (park here for the longer hike-in option). Continue on FR 90 for 1 mile, then turn right into the Middle Falls day-use parking area and hike 0.5 mile on the Lewis River Trail (elevation gain: 225 feet; high point: 1750 feet). **BY TRAIL:** From the Lower Falls (Swim #9) day-use parking area, hike 1.5 miles on the Lewis River Trail (elevation gain: 560 feet; high point: 1750 feet).

The Lewis River waterfalls are absolutely beautiful, with clear water from Mount Adams glacial melt. It's hard to emphasize enough just how stunning the water is, so clear that you can see to the boulders down below. There are two ways to get to the Middle Falls: a short hike or a longer hike from the Lower Falls (Swim #9).

From the Middle Lewis Falls parking lot, it's a 0.5-mile hike to the river that is less steep than the descent to the Lower Falls. For the longer hike, park at the Lower Falls Campground day-use parking lot (Swim #9) and hike 1.5 miles on the wide, mostly flat Lewis River Trail to Middle Falls. This is a beautiful hike along a well-maintained, mossy, and soft trail. If you are camping at the Lower Falls campground, it's a no-brainer to use this trail, but if you have time, we recommend using this hike to check out both falls regardless of where you park.

The Middle Falls, the widest in the area, has a 33-foot drop. From the waterfall the Lewis River flows green between flat rock shores, with tall cedars and firs on either side. There's plenty of room to spread out and absorb heat from the sun-baked rocks. If you see kayakers, you can assume that they are experts—these falls are no joke. Don't risk life and limb by jumping in—simply enjoy the swim below the falls.

There are many other amazing access points along the Lewis River Trail, and exploration would be worthwhile. You can hike the entire trail for an 8.8-mile round-trip. From the Lower Falls Recreation Area, walk 1.5 miles upstream to Middle Lewis River Falls,

Waterfall: Check. Clear water: Check. Lounging rocks: What are you waiting for?

then 2.9 more miles to Quartz Creek trailhead, scouting for other swimming holes along the way. In fact, there are ten or so other waterfalls within 5 miles: Cussed Hollow Falls, Chickoon Creek Falls, Lower Lewis Falls (Swim #9), Lower Cooper Creek Falls, Copper Creek Falls, Middle Lewis Falls, Alec Creek Falls, Upper Lewis Falls, Taitnapum Falls, Lower Quartz Creek Falls, and Tillicum Creek Falls. Visit them all!

 **COUNCIL LAKE**

TYPE: Mountain-forest lake, beach
LOCATION: Roadside in Gifford Pinchot National Forest northeast of Woodland and Cougar via I-5 and SR 503/FR 90
WATER: Cold, clear, deep blue-green
SEASON: Summer through early fall
WHO'S HERE: Kid-friendly, dog-friendly; fisherfolk, campers
AMENITIES: Parking, outhouse, primitive camping, fire rings; fishing
NOTES: Check road conditions, due to many washouts on Forest Service roads in this area in

It's a nice sandy beach on the south end of Council Lake.

2016. Last mile is on good-condition dirt and gravel road, but four-wheel drive recommended.
LOCAL'S TIP: For a very challenging ride with amazing views of the South Cascades,
mountain bike to Council Lake on the 30.5-mile Boundary Trail #1, starting at Bear Meadows.
GPS COORDINATES: 46.2663 N, –121.6317 W

GETTING THERE

FROM THE SOUTH: From I-5 at Woodland, take exit 21 toward Woodland and Cougar and turn right onto Lewis River Road/State Route 503. Drive east on SR 503 through the town of Cougar. The road becomes Forest Road 90 at the Skamania County line. Continue east on FR 90 to a junction with FR 25, at about 47 miles from I-5. Turn right here to stay on FR 90. Cross the North Fork Lewis River and continue up FR 90 for about 14 miles from FR 25, where you pass the Lower Falls Recreation Area (Swim # 9). Continue on FR 90 for another 15 miles, turn left on FR 23, and drive 5 miles to FR 2334. FROM THE NORTH: From US Highway 12 at Randle, go south on SR 131/FR 23/FR 25. After 1 mile, veer left onto FR 23/Cispus Road (check for road closures in this area) and follow it about 6 miles to a fork just before the Cispus River. Stay left on FR 23 for approximately 26 miles to FR 2334. FROM EITHER DIRECTION: Turn west onto FR 2334, drive just over 1 mile, and turn right onto FR 2334-016/Boundary Trail Road. In 0.25 mile reach Council Lake parking.

At 4225 feet elevation, Council Lake is a crystal-clear mountain lake on the northwest side of Mount Adams. Not surprisingly, the air up here is noticeably cooler than farther down below on the Lewis River. Also not surprisingly, the water is equivalently colder. Anglers love this lake and others in the area. That's because it's annually stocked with a variety of fish: rainbow, brook, and brown trout. According to the Washington Department of Fish and Wildlife, the best time for fishing is June through October, which is also when the roads are most likely open.

The last mile or so to get here is a dirt and gravel road in good condition that dead-ends at a free-form parking area at the southwestern tip of the lake, useful for accessing the lake or using the primitive camping spots. Having four-wheel drive might not be a bad idea but isn't 100 percent necessary. You can also park on the side of the road—at least, there are no signs to the contrary. Either way, you'll be parked about 200 feet from the water's edge at most, so find your way down the myriad trails to a nice sandy beach.

The free rustic camping means that you'll likely find yourself among campers, many of whom will be wearing fishing vests and camo. If you camp, bring enough gear to brave fast-changing mountain weather, specifically wind- or thunderstorms, and water-appropriate shoes or sandals in case there's an odd rusting fishhook lying around. The campsites are situated near one another, but the big trees surrounding the lake are like natural privacy dividers. Here you're fairly deep into the woods, without a gas station or grocery store in sight.

If you're here to just swim, be prepared to share the deep blue water with these fisherpeople and their equipment. The wide, sandy beach—a rarity in the Pacific Northwest—provides easy entrance to the water, where anglers can haul their canoes or other fishing boats in and out, and you can launch your floaties or stand-up paddleboards. The water is clean and crisp, too cold to stay in for long. But going between the water and sunshine on the south side of the lake or a fire ring at your campsite is like the PNW's version of the Scandinavian spa ritual. It'll get your blood pumping!

The Ohanapecosh is arguably Washington's most beautiful river. (Swim #17)

MOUNT RAINIER AREA

MOUNT RAINIER CAN BE viewed in all its snow-covered glory from many parts of the state. At more than 14,410 feet above sea level, it is the most glaciated of all the peaks in the United States' Lower 48. Six major rivers are born atop this active volcano, including the Cowlitz and the Ohanapecosh, which provide fine swimming holes. You can make the popular loop around Mount Rainier from west to east and back by taking Interstate 5 to Interstate 90 to Interstate 82, then circling around back to western Washington on US Highway 12/White Pass Scenic Byway.

The other rivers in this chapter—Chehalis, Tilton, Tieton, American, and Green—spring from the foothills and Cascade crest surrounding Rainier. US 12, which runs 124 miles from I-5 just north of Centralia and Chehalis east to Yakima (and continues east through Walla Walla), is one of the lesser-known cross-Cascades passes, yet it is a scenic route from which you can access this region's abundant water.

12 CHEHALIS RIVER: RAINBOW FALLS STATE PARK

TYPE: Lowland river, waterfall, pools, small beach
LOCATION: Roadside in state park west of Chehalis via I-5 and SR 6
WATER: Cold to cool, clearish, cleanish, dark blue
SEASON: Summer through early fall
WHO'S HERE: Kid-friendly, leashed-dog–friendly; campers, families, picnickers, college students, hikers, bikers, horseback riders, RVers
AMENITIES: Parking, restrooms with showers, picnic area, kitchen shelter, grills, campground, RV dump station, ranger station, baseball diamond, fuchsia garden
NOTE: Day-use fee or Discover Pass required
LOCAL'S TIP: Check out the Shankz Black Light Miniature Golf in Chehalis.
GPS COORDINATES: 46.6322 N, –123.2330W

GETTING THERE

NORTH SIDE OF RIVER: From I-5 at Chehalis, take exit 77 for State Route 6 west toward Pe Ell and Raymond. Follow SR 6/Main Street west for 17 miles and turn right onto Chandler Road. Go 0.3 mile and turn right onto Leudinghaus Road. Go 0.8 mile and turn right into Rainbow Falls State Park. Follow signs to the day-use parking area.
SOUTH SIDE OF RIVER: For closer access but without any park facilities, from I-5 at Chehalis, take exit 77 for SR 6 west toward Pe Ell and Raymond. Follow SR 6/Main Street west for 16.4 miles to a pullout on the right on the park's south side.

Rainbow Falls State Park claims 139 acres around the Chehalis River, including 3400 feet of riverfront. Here, in one of the few places untouched by logging in this area, you are surrounded by old-growth forest. Nearby logging businesses are still in operation, though

Bedrock falls, sandy pockets, and a state-protected forest make Rainbow Falls State Park a great place to spend an entire weekend.

they do promise that their methods are sustainable. There are also tree plantations, where trees, planted in perfectly straight rows not seen in natural forests, provide some interesting roadside visuals. If you'd like a real Douglas fir for a Christmas tree, visit in December.

Signage for the state park is a bit vague. Lots of folks access it from State Route 6 (which runs along the south side of the river), probably in part to avoid fees. But of course you'd never take the cheapskate route! The more people who step up and pay the fees—in this case, by purchasing a Discover Pass—the better maintained these parks will be. From the pullout on SR 6, it's a very short walk (100 feet) down the riverbank to the water. The park's hiking trails are located on this side of the river as well; if you want to walk away from the river and out into the forest, the trailhead located underneath a huge Douglas fir connects you to 10 miles of trails: the Oxalis Loop, Deer Trail, Hemlock Trail, Salal Trail, and Woodpecker Trail.

The entrance to the more developed area of the park is located on the north side of the river, off Leudinghaus Road. Here you can find all the amenities, including walk-in campsites, RV sites, and horse camping. This grassy and gorgeous park has the potential to draw a crowd. There's lots of local color, campers, and, because of its 44-mile proximity to Olympia, college kids. If you're lucky, you'll spy a middle-aged person in a tiny Speedo or floral bikini; they might just happen to be a politician taking a well-earned break from their duties at the capital.

From the day-use parking area, it is about 200 feet to the river on various park trails. Canoe access lies west of Rainbow Falls. Despite its being called Rainbow Falls, it'd be a stretch to truly designate it a waterfall. (If you type "Rainbow Falls" into your search engine and get pictures of giant waterfalls, you're probably looking at ones with the same name located in Florida, California, Colorado, Hawaii, North Carolina, Tennessee . . . the list goes on. Apparently this is a popular name.) Maybe at the river's high times, the basalt bedrock ledge could form a 10-foot waterfall. Maybe. Usually it's more like a channel dropping 5 or 6 feet.

If you walk above the falls along the shore, you'll find flat water with deeper pools interspersed with shallow ones—head downstream for truer swimming spots, but be careful not to get washed down the falls. If you're downstream of the falls, you could swim up into the falls, using common sense about risk per usual. The bedrock ledge juts into the river off the shoreline, and solid rock meets water with nothing in between. Though there are no cliff jumps, you can jump off from the shore. At times, it's hard to tell the water depth, so collect some intel before taking that leap.

When you're ready for some lounge time, settle down on one of the sand pockets between the bedrock, a minibeach for little kiddos to play on. The strapping old-growth trees provide a shelter of green, and they tend to be far enough from the shore that they don't cast shadows on the river until late afternoon.

13 TILTON RIVER: AT MORTON

TYPE: Lowland river, pools
LOCATION: Roadside outside Morton via US 12, SR 7, and SR 508
WATER: Cold to cool, clearish, cleanish, blue-green
SEASON: Summer and early fall
WHO'S HERE: Kid-friendly, dog-friendly; lots of folks who work in the area's agricultural zone, local kids, old loggers, anglers
AMENITIES: Picnic tables, food, and lodging nearby
LOCAL'S TIP: Into hang-gliding? It will take some digging, but you can probably find someone to take you on a flight from nearby Dog Mountain, east of Morton, where you can catch a breathtaking view of Mount St. Helens, Mount Hood, and Mount Rainier.
GPS COORDINATES: 46.5607 N, –122.2845 W

GETTING THERE

From I-5 south of Chehalis, take exit 68 onto US Highway 12 east toward Morton and Yakima. In 31 miles turn left (north) onto State Route 7 into Morton. In about 0.6 mile, turn left (west) onto SR 508/Main Avenue. After 0.6 mile, arrive at the bridge over the Tilton; park on the road shoulder.

Located right on the edge of the old logging town of Morton, the Tilton River swimming hole is unexpected—and that's part of its charm. Whether you're coming from or going to Mount Rainier along US Highway 12, the White Pass Scenic Byway, or taking a day to explore the cozy town of Morton, this tucked-away little swim spot is right off US 12 and nearby Interstate 5, making it easy to access for a quick dip.

The river is a decent size—neither a teeny creek nor overly raging. During the high-water times of early summer, beware the risk of whitewater rapids and wait until the water goes down before getting in.

From the bridge, walk 100 feet or so down to the shore, where there's a lot of cool river geology—features that make this roadside spot worth visiting. Within the river and along the shore there's some nice bedrock, situated to form two pools. The rocks aren't big enough for cliff jumping, but they're just the right size for a 1- to 2-foot leap into the water.

Right under the bridge there's a man-made boulder (meaning: chunk of concrete), and you might just spot an angler throwing a line. The Tilton River is a popular spot for fisherfolk; since the construction of the Mayfield Dam in the 1960s, the Cowlitz Salmon Hatchery and the Cowlitz Trout Hatchery truck their fish in for release in the Tilton River, so you will be sharing this spot with locals looking for a fresh catch.

A calm day on the Tilton River

Be sure to check out the pools just downstream from the bridge and the excellent spot 50 feet or so upstream of the bridge, where a rocky beach transitions into a big pool. This is adjacent to Gus Backstrom City Park, which includes a couple of picnic tables on a grassy knoll. When the water is low at the end of summer, you can put an inner tube in at the park and float a short way down to that big bottom pool. Though this roadside swimming hole is small, it has a lot going for it. Poke around and see what you find. Tilton River is worth exploring if you have the time.

14 JOHNSON CREEK–GLACIER CREEK

TYPE: Mountain forest creek, small pool
LOCATION: Roadside west of Packwood via US 12 and FR 21
WATER: Cold, clear, clean, blue-green
SEASON: Summer through early fall

Keep an eye out for hidden but accessible gems like this one at Johnson Creek.

WHO'S HERE: Kid-friendly, dog-friendly; people in the know
AMENITIES: DIY camping; food and lodging nearby
LOCAL'S TIP: Car-camp here for free, but there's only one spot so get here early.
GPS COORDINATES: 46.5399 N, –121.6238 W

GETTING THERE

From I-5 south of Chehalis, take exit 68 onto US 12 east toward Packwood. After 62 miles, turn right (south) onto unpaved Forest Road 21. Stay right to stay on this road, then after 4.3 miles, turn right onto FR 2115. Drive another 0.2 mile and park at the road's end.

This is one of those spots that we found unexpectedly while driving along Forest Road 21, just west of the Goat Rocks Wilderness. Johnson Creek is way down below in the valley and not observable from the road, but you can see the turnoff. From the road's dead end, walk the well-beaten trail down about 200 feet to the water, near where Glacier Creek flows into Johnson Creek.

And there you'll find a small, shallow swimming hole with just enough depth to submerge in. Beside its pretty clear green water, the big cedar and maple trees shade ferns all along the shore. You'll also find some nice rocks to lizard out on when the sun is high in the sky. There is one nice little DYI campsite right on the shore, and this would be a great place to call home for a night or two.

One of the main reasons this swimming hole is included is to show you, dear reader, how keeping an eye out for nondescript or undocumented swimming holes and exploring for yourself can pay off. Wherever the road meets the water in this beautiful Pacific Northwest, you're more than likely to find something worth checking out. And let us know what gems you find.

 ## 15 COWLITZ RIVER: LA WIS WIS

TYPE: Mountain-forest river, beach
LOCATION: Roadside in Gifford Pinchot National Forest east of Packwood via US 12 near SR 123
WATER: Very cold, crystal clear, very clean, emerald green
SEASON: Summer through fall
WHO'S HERE: Kid-friendly, dog-friendly; fisherfolk, recreationists in the know, local families with kids, good mix
AMENITIES: Rope swing; campground nearby

LOCAL'S TIP: Go to Paradise in Mount Rainier National Park to see where all this beautiful water comes from.
GPS COORDINATES: 46.6643 N, −121.6002 W

GETTING THERE

From I-5 south of Chehalis, take exit 68 onto US Highway 12. After 69 miles, turn left (north) onto Forest Road 1270, 2.6 miles west of State Route 123. After 0.6 mile, reach the road's end and park (if it's a busy summer day, you might have to back out when it's time to go).

This swimming hole on the Cowlitz River, located just downstream of the La Wis Wis Campground, sits right outside Mount Rainier National Park on the peak's southeast flanks. It's not in the park, so no permits are needed. But if you are stopping here, you probably already have your pass, since there's a good chance you are coming from or going to Mount Rainier. It's located right off US Highway 12, so stop by on the way to or from White Pass or Yakima to the east. This highway runs by various bodies of water between the Cowlitz River and Yakima: Clear Fork Cowlitz River, Lily Lake, Leech Lake, South Fork Clear Creek, Dog Lake, Clear Lake, Rimrock Lake, Tieton River, and Naches River. Not to mention the plethora of lakes and rivers to the west.

Finding clarity on the Cowlitz River

From the end of the road, walk 30 or 40 feet to the riverbed. Not surprisingly, the river is a gorgeous deep turquoise green like others in the area, with big moss-covered rocks along the shore. Exposed to long hours of sun, this open part of the river is so clear that you can see way down into its depths. The sunlight shines a spotlight on the rocks—the bed is quite cobblestoned, so bring your water shoes or river sandals (unless you have well-calloused feet). No matter the time of year, the Cowlitz is always really cold—even in the hottest days of summer, this is an in-and-out kind of spot that will make your teeth chatter.

You enter on river left, and across the river a small rope swing carries the minimally brave out over the water. You have to swim to get to it, as well as to the decent jumping-off rocks and a sandy beach. This is a flat, broad stretch of river; harness your salmon-powers to swim upstream against the current, which will get you into a small canyon.

 ## 16 NORTH FORK TIETON RIVER: BELOW CLEAR LAKE DAM

TYPE: Mountain-forest river, pool
LOCATION: Short walk in Okanogan–Wenatchee National Forest east of White Pass via US 12 and FR 1200
WATER: Cold to cool, clearish, cleanish, blue-green
SEASON: Summer into fall
WHO'S HERE: Kid-friendly, dog-friendly; Boy and Girl Scouts, campers, RVers, anglers
AMENITIES: Parking, restrooms, campgrounds, picnic area, boat ramp
NOTE: Northwest Forest Pass required
LOCAL'S TIP: Reserve the Clear Lake Campground group site, which accesses the best part of the swimming hole, and turn it into a party.
GPS COORDINATES: 46.6291 N, –121.2714 W

GETTING THERE

On US Highway 12 at White Pass, drive east 7.7 miles and turn right onto Forest Road 1200/Tieton Reservoir Road. After 0.2 mile, make a slight left onto FR 740/ Clear Lake Road. After 0.5 mile, just before the road makes a sharp right turn, arrive at a big pullout parking area on the left.

Immediately below Clear Lake, a small dam was built using a mix of natural rock and concrete. This channelizes the water of the North Fork Tieton River, and the spillway creates a lovely swimming hole. The dam itself has no controls, so the spillway has more water during peak runoff time. Though this area is part of what's called Clear Lake, in essence it is a river with current. Don't let the man-made aspect of Clear Lake Outflow turn you off—get in where you can!

Is that sun really warm enough for a swim?

This area is far enough off US Highway 12 that you don't hear or smell the traffic, but it's still a busy place, with many campgrounds and youth camps giving the area a summer-camp feel. It chills out quite a bit during the week. The drive from the highway is nearly all paved, with a well-maintained dirt road at the end that is RV-friendly. Once you park, you are very close to the water; walk about 0.1 mile downstream for the best spot.

You'd think that an outflow wouldn't be all that big, and at first that seems to be the case with this spot. But once you get over the spillway, you'll find a pretty big pool, with lots of room to swim around. There's no true cliff jump or anything like that, but there are plenty of rocks to lizard out on. Since it's easy to get to and the slowness of the current reduces the risk of being swept away, bring your stand-up paddleboard or floaties.

A day-use picnic area is a little bit farther in on Forest Road 740, and there's one campsite right on the river a bit downstream of the swim spot. Clear Lake group site is located on river left, the side with more protruding rocks and a steeper shoreline and therefore better to jump from. River right is the side from which more people access the water. If the outflow is too high, you can skip the river and instead walk up to Clear Lake from the parking area. Lots of fisherfolk do.

17 OHANAPECOSH RIVER: CAMPGROUND BRIDGE

TYPE: Mountain-forest river, minor whitewater, small beach
LOCATION: Roadside in Mount Rainier National Park via southeast entrance at SR 123
WATER: Very cold, very clear, very clean, emerald green
SEASON: Midsummer to early fall
WHO'S HERE: Kid-friendly; campers, hikers, retirees, families
AMENITIES: Parking, restrooms and outhouses, drinking water, campground, fire rings, RV dump station, Ohanapecosh Visitors Center
NOTE: Park entrance fee or National Park Pass required
LOCAL'S TIP: Go down to the nearby Cowlitz River (Swim #15), which is similar and less crowded. And it's free.
GPS COORDINATES: 46.7361 N, –121.5663 W

A Northwest gem!

The Ohanapecosh is touted as one of the most beautiful rivers in Washington. Right inside the Mount Rainier National Park southeast boundary, it flows off Rainier's Ohanapecosh Glacier and travels 16 miles to the Cowlitz River just south of La Wis Wis. The Ohaney, as it's nicknamed, is in the middle of nature though not unpeopled, with Rainier National Park's Ohanapecosh Visitors Center and big, beautiful campground connected by a bridge over the water. Reserve a campsite for sometime in July through early August—plan to stay an entire weekend or more if you can swing it.

This area is not the flattest part of the river, and there's even some minor whitewater. That's OK when the volume is low, but when it's high, you do not want to end up floating downstream—where you'd find yourself in some serious Class IV and V rapids! Per usual: when in doubt, stay out. Keep to the zone near the bridge.

From the parking areas on either side of the bridge, you are 100 feet or so from the bridge and the river. Take your pick: river left has a small sand beach; river right has a rockier shoreline and some bigger rocks to jump off of into the water. Sometimes there's also a fallen log to walk on. This area is great for swimming or lounging in a small flotation device; there's plenty of room to swim, and the water is superclear, sometimes a spectacular turquoise, and icy cold year round.

The river is pristine, but chances of being here by yourself are low—there are 188 individual campsites and 2 group campsites in this section of the park alone. If you prefer solitude and don't mind a crisper dip, go at the bookends of the season. Because the area has been protected from logging and major resource extraction, the campground is situated within a towering old-growth forest of western red cedar, Douglas fir, and western hemlock. Most sunshine is filtered through this sprawling green canopy, so swim between 11:00 a.m. and 3:00 p.m. for peak exposure.

There's lots to do on land as well. Walk the 1.3-mile Grove of the Patriarchs Trail, the 3-mile Silver Falls Trail, or the 1-mile Ohanacopesh Hot Springs Trail. This last trail will take you to the hot springs, but don't get your hopes up—they are no longer in use. (And, as the National Park Service reminds us: Don't be a meadow stomper. Stay on the trails.) If you happen to get caught in a surprise rainstorm and/or if you want to learn a thing or two, step inside the visitors center to look over the 3D topographical map of the park or purchase a book on the rich history of the area. Check out the many great trails to explore in other parts of the park.

The perfect summer day: Wake up at the campground, make campfire coffee and breakfast, go for a hike, get back in time for a swim during the hottest hours of the day, cook some weenies over the fire for dinner, and then turn in. Sounds heavenly, doesn't it?

 ## 18 AMERICAN RIVER

TYPE: Mountain-forest river
LOCATION: Roadside in Okanogan–Wenatchee National Forest east of Chinook Pass via SR 410
WATER: Cold, clear, clean, blue-green
SEASON: Summer into fall
WHO'S HERE: Kid-friendly, dog-friendly; campers, anglers, RVers
AMENITIES: Campgrounds, parking, outhouses, drinking water
NOTE: Northwest Forest Pass required
LOCAL'S TIP: To go on a self-directed swimming-hole exploration, simply drive along SR 410, the Chinook Pass Highway, and keep your eyes peeled.
GPS COORDINATES: 46.9259 N, –121.3661 W

GETTING THERE

From State Route 167 between Puyallup and Sumner, take SR 410 east 15 miles to Enumclaw. Continue east on SR 410 through Greenwater and after 23.4 miles, at the junction with SR 123 at Cayuse Pass, keep left onto Mather Memorial Parkway to

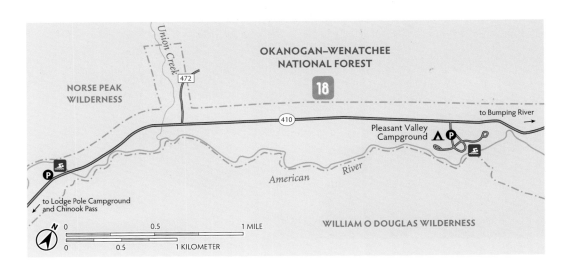

Chinook Pass. After 8.7 miles, turn left onto an unmarked road just before crossing the American River and find a parking area right along the river with a nice pool and some DIY camping. Or continue downriver on SR 410 for 2.9 miles to Pleasant Valley Campground on the right for another option.

The American River begs to be swum in. East of the Cascades, State Route 410 weaves roughly alongside the river from Lodge Pole Campground for almost 40 miles to where it joins the Tieton River at US Highway 12 to become the Naches River. Several spots along this stretch are worth visiting—truly, there is no one go-to place, because just about everywhere you land along the American River's shore you'll find clean and clear green water flowing on by. The shore is rocky, with the usual evergreens lining either side. This part of Washington is drier than the infamously wet west side, so the trees around here tend to be smaller and the air less humid. There's lots of car camping, lots of folks fishing rainbow and brown trout, lots of people driving their small RVs up from Yakima.

Though this river does not run from drainage off Mount Rainier, it's close to The Mountain as the crow flies. Along the way from Chinook Pass downriver are many places

The American River near the Union Creek Sno-Park

The American River near the Paradise Valley Campground

to swim and camp: Lodge Pole Campground, Pleasant Valley Campground, Salmon Cove group site, Hells Crossing Campground, Pine Needle group site. Most of these butt right up against the river. The American Forks Campground marks the spot where the American River meets the Bumping River.

There are frequent pullouts along the highway where you can park and then walk a few feet to the water. Usually the parking is limited, so you'll still have a secluded feeling. And if that's not happening, you can always drive down the road to find another spot. It's perfect for those driving over Chinook Pass from western Washington to the east side of the crest, or vice versa.

The two spots noted on our map—an unmarked pullout at a DIY campsite downriver from Lodge Pole Campground, and Pleasant Valley Campground—aren't superfeatured; they have pebbly shorelines with a bit of sand here and there. The water is just deep enough to swim in, which is consistent with other swimming spots you'll find along the river: it just sort of pools up. Tubing is not recommended because many downed trees occasionally and randomly jut out into or cross the river.

Just west of the confluence of the American and Bumping rivers (about 40 miles west of the town of Naches), the American River guard station is available for rent. A converted summer residence and worksite built by the men of the 932nd Camp Naches Civilian Conservation Corps crew, the cabin is a locus of all kinds of activities: fishing and boating in Bumping Lake, hiking and horseback riding in the William O. Douglas and Norse Peak wilderness areas on either side of the river, and snowshoeing and cross-country skiing during the winter months.

Near Hells Crossing Campground, the Goat Creek trailhead (46.9641 N, –121.2675 W) leads to Goat Peak at 6473 feet elevation on American Ridge, a 6.5-mile round-trip with 3200 feet of elevation gain and stunning views of Goat Rocks, Bumping Lake, Mount Rainier, Fifes Peak, and the Stuart Range. There are tons of outdoor activities in this area worth checking out, then following up with a refreshing dip in this cold, slow-flowing river.

 GREEN RIVER GORGE

TYPE: Lowland river, current
LOCATION: Hike-in in Green River Gorge Conservation Area between Black Diamond and Enumclaw via SR 169
WATER: Cold to cool, clearish, clean, blue-green
SEASON: Summer into fall
WHO'S HERE: Kid-friendly, dog-friendly; locals

AMENITIES: Food and lodging nearby

LOCAL'S TIP: Do you love to fly remote-control airplanes? Then check out Flaming Geyser State Park, roughly 8 miles downstream. There's a specially designated area just for that.

GPS COORDINATES: 47.2831 N, –121.9650 W (parking); 47.2908 N, –121.9728 W (swimming hole)

GETTING THERE

From I-405 in Renton, take exit 4 and merge onto State Route 169 east through Maple Valley to Black Diamond. Drive 22 miles past Black Diamond and turn left onto Enumclaw–Franklin Road SE. This paved but potholed road is not very well maintained, but any two-wheel-drive car could navigate it. After 2.4 miles, reach a small pullout at a red gate on the left side of the road, with enough room for three or four cars on one side and a couple cars on the other (Note: it's not formal parking.) Enter the unmarked trail here and hike 0.7 mile; (elevation gain: 310 feet; high point: 740 feet).

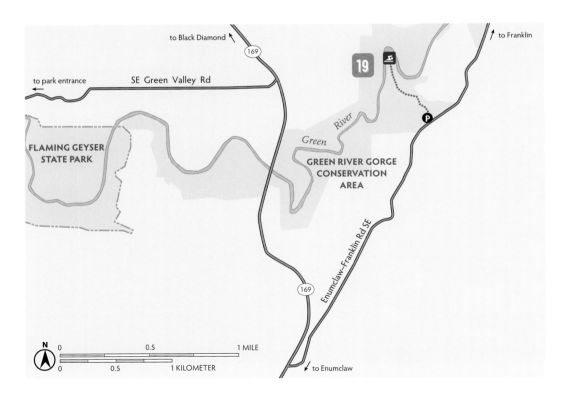

The lazy river current of the Green River

Rather than flowing off Mount Rainier like the other rivers in this chapter, Green River originates from the Cascade crest closer to Interstate 90. (We list it here in the Mount Rainier chapter because it is close to State Route 410, which provides access to Mount Rainier, so there's a good chance potential swimmers might stop by this quiet little swimming hole coming from or going to the mountain.) The Green River Gorge makes a nearly equilateral triangle with Tacoma and Seattle, being 30 miles due east from the former and 40 miles southeast from the latter. Because of urban flooding in the past, it is controlled by Howard A. Hanson Dam, built in 1961. You might have more success here earlier in the season, since the water levels will be lower than on undammed rivers. And, another plus, no fees or passes are required. On the flip side, it's probably too low for kayaking in the summer. Also, no bonus features like restrooms or picnic tables.

From the parking spot, the hike alongside the old chain-link fence is on a relatively easy downhill trail (meaning that it's uphill on the way back). In inclement weather, it can get a little slippery, so be prepared. The 0.7-mile walk is pleasant but not pristine; if you time it right you might just find some wild blackberries and raspberries. Due to logging, at first you walk through scrappy forest, but as you get closer to the river, the trail starts to pitch among big, more mature cedars. Once down into the valley, the trail flattens out as it opens out into the riverbed. The ground is mostly cobble and river rock, so make sure you've got sturdy footwear.

At the river, you'll be inside a big horseshoe as the river does a U-turn around you. This unique shape makes the area feel bigger than it is and offers three distinct zones to set up in. The shrubbery around the water's edge offers some privacy—from one side of the horseshoe you can't see people on the other side. If you decide to spend some time on the shore—sometimes people pack down a hibachi grill and lawn chairs—you'll notice that behind you is forest and out in front on the other side of the river a cliff looms up, then slopes down in either direction to meet the forest. The cliff can block the sun at times, though the light in the afternoon is pretty good, and different parts of the horseshoe catch different amounts of sunshine at different times of day.

The water is deep, with just the right amount of current to swim against. Swim across the river to the river-right side to get to a 3-foot-high rock for some relatively mellow rock jumping. As you work upriver, you'll run into little ripples of whitewater, and if the water level is low enough and, after careful onsite determination, you decide that it's safe, you could hop on an inner tube or strap on a flotation toy and let the current swing you around the bend, then get out on the other side without going too far beyond that. It's a short walk between those two spots, so you could do that fun little mini-tubing adventure over and over.

Classic "horsetail-form" falls (Swim #24)

OLYMPIC PENINSULA

THERE IS A MYSTIQUE to the Olympic Peninsula. Though it is close to Pugetopolis as the crow flies, it tends to be less visited than the Cascades, since it is harder to get to—you either have to take a Washington State ferry or drive Interstate 5 through Tacoma and/or Olympia. The peninsula is incredibly diverse in terms of environment and weather, with glaciated mountains and rain forests, lakes and rivers, Hood Canal and the Strait of Juan de Fuca, and the Pacific Ocean.

 ## 20 SPOON CREEK FALLS

TYPE: Mountain-forest creek, waterfall, pool, small beach
LOCATION: Hike-in in Olympic National Forest west of Olympia via US Highway 101 and SR 8/US 12
WATER: Cold, clear, clean, blue-green
SEASON: Summer and fall
WHO'S HERE: Kid-friendly, dog-friendly; Olympic National Park visitors in the know, locals from Olympia and Centralia
AMENITIES: Camping nearby
NOTE: Northwest Forest Pass required
LOCAL'S TIP: Wear your water shoes—or hiking boots you don't mind getting wet—since you will be getting your feet wet. While you're at it, bring your goggles.
GPS COORDINATES: 47.3540 N, –123.5650 W

GETTING THERE

From I-5 in Olympia, take exit 104 for US Highway 101 north and drive 5.9 miles. Keep left onto State Route 8 west and follow signs for Montesano and Aberdeen. Drive for 32 miles, passing through Elma, where SR 8 joins US Highway 12, then exit right for Devonshire Road west of Montesano. After 0.2 mile, take a slight left onto Wynoochee Valley Road and continue for 33 miles. Turn right onto Forest Road

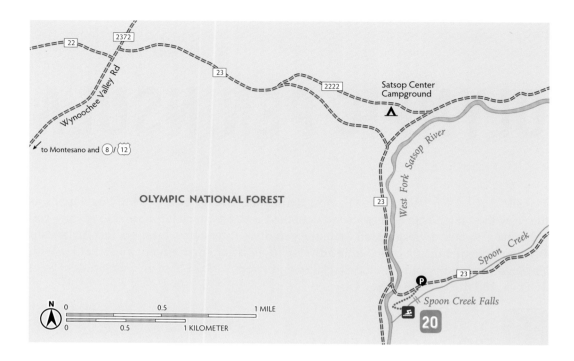

23 before you reach Wynoochee Lake, then go southeast for 2.4 miles. Turn left at a junction to stay on FR 23 across the West Fork Satsop River, continue 0.1 mile, and park on the shoulder, which has room for five or so cars. Hike the unmarked but obvious trail 0.25 mile (elevation gain: 180 feet; high point: 1000 feet).

Spoon Creek Falls is near the southern tip of Olympic National Park—not in the park but a few miles south of it. Nearby Wynoochee Lake is better known and more traversed, with its many campsites, calm and canoe-able waters, and 12- to 16-mile trail loop, depending on the height of the Wynoochee River. It is worth visiting for the day or for some overnight camping, but if you want to get in the water at a spot that is a little quieter, Spoon Creek Falls is a better bet. To get there you drive mostly on paved roads and well-maintained dirt. You'll be a long way from the bigger highways, so you probably won't see anyone biking or walking along the road.

Most people would hike this short unmarked trail simply for the views of the waterfall. The hike is short, surrounded by sprawling, large second-growth hemlock and cedar. It's downhill all the way, so don't be surprised to find it uphill all the way back. Regardless, it's pretty easy traveling coming and going. Before the falls is a confluence—the West Fork Satsop River and Spoon Creek—where you can look down into pristine, clear water. If you are in the mood for an adventure, you could wander around to find your own private pool somewhere. From the lookout point, the trail switchbacks in the other direction and takes you down to Spoon Creek, where, after a short distance, you come around a corner to find the gorgeous Spoon Creek Falls.

The waterfall is not huge but it lends itself well to photographs. There are two excellent choices here. The first is a one-person ice Jacuzzi—well aerated, with lots of little bubbles—like a swimmable pothole practically underneath the waterfall, about 40 feet down from the top. You can even get under the waterfall—of course, make sure that the flow is low first.

After this pool the waterfall takes a 10-foot spill into option two, a larger pool with calmer crystal-clear waters where you can see right through to the rocky bottom. The pool is decently though not extremely cold and not very deep, so wade in from the

Feeling small at Spoon Creek Falls

gravelly beach rather than jump or dive. You can swim laps, paddle around, or float on an inflatable of your choice in this pool. Across the outflow is a little beach, and there's a log or two where you can sit or hang your towels. All in all, a special little Olympic Peninsula spot.

 # LAKE CUSHMAN: BIG ROCK

TYPE: Lowland-forest reservoir, cliff jump
LOCATION: Roadside in Olympic National Forest west of Hoodsport via US 101 on Hood Canal
WATER: Cold to cool, clear, cleanish, blue-green
SEASON: Year-round if you are up for cold water
WHO'S HERE: Sunburnt drunk people, high schoolers, college students, boaters
AMENITIES: Camping nearby
LOCAL'S TIP: Get here early or on a cooler day to avoid crowds and get an awesome Instagram photo.
GPS COORDINATES: 47.4955 N, –123.3018 W

GETTING THERE

From US Highway 101 between Shelton and Quilcene, drive to Hoodsport and turn west onto State Route 119. After 9.2 miles, turn left to stay on SR 119/North Lake Cushman Road. After 4.6 miles, reach the Big Rock area on SR 119/North Lake Cushman Road and park on the roadside.

We usually shy away from reservoirs, which are generally defined as being a portion of a dammed-up river, versus a natural lake. This is a fairly flimsy categorization, because oftentimes bodies of water are mislabeled as lakes when they are, in fact, reservoirs. Lake Cushman is a good example: a reservoir that is quite large, as big as natural Lakes Crescent and Quinault. Usually reservoirs are not as clean as natural lakes because the dam restricts outflow, and sometimes a little film can develop on the water surface. Of course, this depends on how water is released. In terms of quality, Lake Cushman is one notch up from Lake Washington—not totally pristine, but without algae or urban pollution.

Lake Cushman has tons of places to swim. Some of the shoreline is private property, but there are plenty of public access points, including lots of little tucked-away spots along the side of North Lake Cushman Road. This swim's spot, Big Rock, gets its name because . . . it's a big rock. Surely someone knows whether this big rock has held residence forever or is a result of a construction project way back when. Either way, the really giant rock makes for great cliff jumping. The boulder itself is quite large, with room for, at a guess, up to thirty people. The water is deep, at least deep enough for the maximum jump height

The Big Rock in Lake Cushman is, well . . . big, and makes for great jumping, diving, or just hanging out.

of around 17 feet. Shorter jumping-off points are around 10 feet or so, which is not terribly dangerous but still nothing to sneeze at.

To conquer the Big Rock, you have to climb over lots of little boulders along the road, then balance your way over to its base. Sometimes there's a rope or two that you can use to hand-over-hand up the rock face. Make sure you assess the quality of the rope before using it—check for weathering, tears, etc. Use any ropes you find at your own risk. You can also boulder up, but be sure you know what you're doing.

Big Rock is a popular spot, and it does fill up. This is not somewhere to go if you want peace and quiet. It's a scene, truly—on a hot summer weekend, it's like an MTV spring-break reality-TV show. (Do these still exist?) On the busiest days, you can join a crowd of

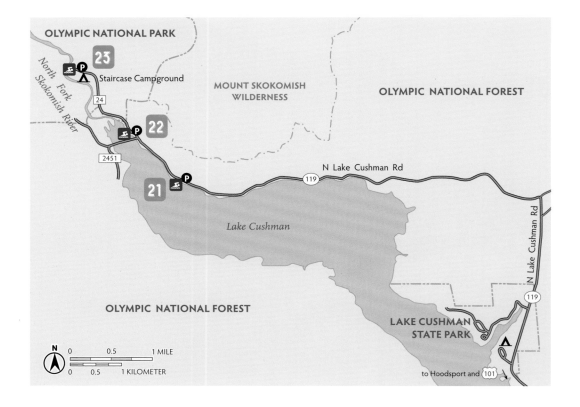

100-odd partying high school and college kids by parking alongside the forty or so cars crammed on the side of the road. Total party scene, if that's what you're into: Jeep tops down, motorboats cruising by, a multitude of stereos blaring—like the logboom on Lake Washington for Seafair's hydroplane races.

Now, there are other options. The more tranquil times are the off hours. Around sunrise happens to be the best time for photos; a little online research will yield some beautiful sunrise Big Rock pics from both famous and novice photographers and Instagrammers. (In fact, we found out about this spot on Instagram. The photos are amazing.) If you want to get a head start, rent a cabin at Lake Cushman Resort or stay at one of the many campgrounds in the area, such as Lake Cushman State Park.

If you come later in the day and want to avoid the crowds, from the access point described above, you can walk west to find a quieter place to enter the water. However, the rocks there are smaller to swim out to, climb up, and jump from. The summer party scene evaporates in the off season, if you're up for a polar plunge. One more item to note: most people who come here for the cliff jumping stay for the hookup culture.

22 LAKE CUSHMAN: NORTHEAST SHORE

TYPE: Lowland-forest reservoir, beach
LOCATION: Roadside in Olympic National Forest west of Hoodsport via US 101 on Hood Canal
WATER: Cold to cool, clear, cleanish, blue-green
SEASON: Year-round
WHO'S HERE: Kid-friendly, dog-friendly; families, picnickers
AMENITIES: Parking, outhouse; camping nearby
LOCAL'S TIP: Bring your stand-up paddleboard.
GPS COORDINATES: 47.5036 N, −123.3136 W

The beach and day-use area on the northeast shore of Lake Cushman

From US Highway 101 between Shelton and Quilcene, drive to Hoodsport and turn west onto State Route 119. After 9.2 miles, turn left to stay on SR 119/North Lake Cushman Road. After 5.4 miles, arrive at the day-use area on SR 119/North Lake Cushman Road and park (there's room for twenty-five or so cars).

On the northeast corner of Lake Cushman, the road parallels the water, so you can just park anywhere and swim. However, as on any big body of water, there can be lots of chop on windy days. Normally a spot like this isn't that impressive, but it's protected from the wind and chop, and it's such a nice alternative to the party scene at Big Rock (Swim #21). To get away from the Big Rock crowd, drive 0.8 mile west. (You could do some cliff jumping at Big Rock first, then come here to chill out, or send your teenagers up to Big Rock while you read your book undisturbed on the shore here.)

Right before you get to this little area, Forest Road 2451 goes left across the lake to the head of the reservoir, where the North Fork Skokomish River flows in. For the most part this road is built up on a spit, but there's also a bit of a bridge to let the water flow through underneath. The spit can block the wind to create a calm zone, and over the years logs have washed down and gotten pushed into a corner to form a fun little feature.

At this established beach (also known as Bear Gulch Picnic Site), you park roughly 20 feet from the water's edge, so access is supereasy. Launch your stand-up paddleboard here, and bring a cooler and post a sun tent if you want to stay all day.

23 NORTH FORK SKOKOMISH RIVER: STAIRCASE TRAILHEAD

TYPE: Lowland-forest river, small rapids, beach
LOCATION: Short walk-in in Olympic National Park, west of Hoodsport via US 101 on Hood Canal
WATER: Cold, clear, clean, turquoise
SEASON: Summer
WHO'S HERE: Kid-friendly; families, hikers, campers
AMENITIES: Parking, restrooms, picnic area, campground, ranger station, wheelchair-accessible trail
NOTE: Park entrance fee or National Park Pass required
LOCAL'S TIP: Go to this lesser-known entrance to Olympic National Park to experience the park without the crowds.
GPS COORDINATES: 47.5158 N, –123.3300 W

Clear green waters and beginner tubing on North Fork Skokomish River

GETTING THERE

From US Highway 101 between Shelton and Quilcene, drive to Hoodsport and turn west onto State Route 119. After 9.2 miles, turn left to stay on SR 119/North Lake Cushman Road. After 5.4 miles continue straight as the road becomes Forest Road 24/North Staircase Road. After 1.3 miles, park at Staircase trailhead.

Just 1.3 miles north of Lake Cushman, the Staircase trailhead is located at the southeast corner of Olympic National Park. Despite the Staircase Trail being popular, this side of the park and this entrance tend to see fewer visitors than Hurricane Ridge on the north side, near Port Angeles and Lake Crescent, or the Hoh Rain Forest, Quinault Rain Forest, and Quinault River on the southwest side. That has its advantages, especially for those who prefer fewer people without losing easy access.

Park at the Staircase trailhead and walk clockwise a mere 0.1 mile on the mellow Staircase Rapids Loop—which, when in top condition, is wheelchair accessible—to the wooden bridge over the North Fork Skokomish River. Below the bridge is a wide sand-and-rock beach on either side of the river. There's plenty of room on both sides, but the side closer to the ranger station—river left—has old-growth Douglas firs that provide shade, while river right is more open to the sun.

Get into this big, calm stretch of featureless water, which is a clean, clear turquoise and just deep enough to swim. Bring a flotation device and walk 100 feet or so upstream to ride the little rapids right above the bridge. These are small enough to be useful for teaching your kids about tubing fun (and safety).

There are lots of other swimming holes waiting to be found—remember, now, this is Washington, so you can choose your own adventure. You could camp at Staircase and then continue on the 4-mile Staircase Rapids Loop, a favorite among trail runners, or check out other trails—2-mile-long Four Stream and 1-mile-long Shady Lane are on the easier side. For more serious hikers, there's the infamous 5.8-mile round-trip hike to Wagonwheel Lake, reputed to be one of the steepest hikes in Washington; the moderate 15.4-mile round-trip hike to Flapjack Lakes; and the 27-mile round-trip North Fork Skokomish River Trail. Whatever you choose, you will find other golden opportunities to get in the water.

 # ROCKY BROOK FALLS

TYPE: Lowland creek, waterfall, pool
LOCATION: Walk-in near Olympic National Forest near Brinnon via US 101 on Hood Canal
WATER: Cool, clear, clean, blue-green
SEASON: Summer to early fall
WHO'S HERE: Kid-friendly, dog-friendly; families, retirees, waterfall lovers
AMENITIES: Camping nearby

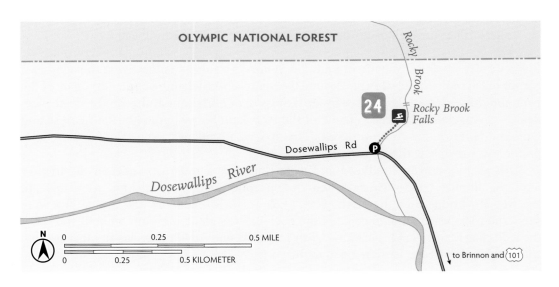

NOTE: Northwest Forest Pass required
LOCAL'S TIP: Stop by Quil Bean Espresso in the town of Quilcene for a cuppa joe.
GPS COORDINATES: 47.7189 N, –122.9435 W (parking); 47.7210 N, –122.9416 W (swimming hole)

GETTING THERE

From US Highway 101 at Brinnon, 26 miles north of Hoodsport and 11 miles south of Quilcene, turn west onto Dosewallips Road. After 3 miles, park on either shoulder and walk about 0.1 mile along the trail (elevation gain: 50 feet; high point: 200 feet).

Tour the Olympic Peninsula or hike in Olympic National Park, then stop by Rocky Brook Falls for a swim. It's off the beaten path just enough to be away from the crowds and your car, but not so far off that it takes all day to get here.

From the roadside parking spot, it's a pretty short walk along the brook to this waterfall. It's a pleasant stretch, almost making you wish it was longer when all of a sudden you are there, having gained only 50 feet or so in elevation. You'll be among other

All are welcome at Rocky Brook Falls.

waterfall aficionados, a handful of whom will be there just to see the gorgeous cascading "horsetail-form" waterfall rather than to swim. That said, the area is not huge, and you will be sharing the gravelly beach and larger rocks. If you bring a dog, be respectful of nearby folks and don't let your pet shake off on top of their picnic blanket (this means you, Huxley el Jefe).

At the base of the waterfall is a pool, with a shallow natural entrance on river right that gets deeper toward the rock face. A couple rocks jut out far enough to hop off of, though it can't be called cliff jumping. The pool is deep enough for swimming, but not all that deep, so double-check before taking a leap. A big log might be lazily floating, great for kids to play on as their parents watch from shore. Grownups could play on it too. The water is crystal clear, so bring a snorkel and mask.

Looking up at the waterfall, to the right is a bushwhacked trail that takes you up to a scree field. You might notice a few rock-climbing bolts beside the waterfall, which don't look overly used, but obviously someone was motivated enough to install them. If you walk up to the top for excellent photo ops, be really careful to (a) not fall off the waterfall and (b) not kick any of the loose rocks down into the pool by accident.

 ## LAKE CRESCENT: BARNES POINT

TYPE: Lowland-forest lake
LOCATION: Hike-in in Olympic National Park west of Port Angeles via US 101
WATER: Very cold, very clear, gorgeous tropical blue-green
SEASON: Year-round
WHO'S HERE: Kid-friendly, dog-friendly; everyone . . . and yet it's quiet
AMENITIES: Parking, food, and lodging at Lake Crescent Lodge and Log Cabin Resort; picnic areas, picnic tables, fire pits, restrooms and outhouses along lakeshore at Lapoel, Bovees Meadow, Fairholme, and northeast shore; fishing, boating, kayaking, hiking nearby, some wheelchair access; camping nearby, including Fairholme Campground; food nearby, including Fairholme Store
NOTE: Park entrance fee or National Park Pass required
LOCAL'S TIP: Bring your snorkel gear. Because of the lack of plant life in the water, you can see up to 60 feet and might catch sight of two kinds of trout—Beardslee and Crescenti— that call Lake Crescent, and only Lake Crescent, home.
GPS COORDINATES: 48.0571 N, –123.7999 W

 ### GETTING THERE

From US Highway 101/North Lincoln Street in Port Angeles, drive west on US 101 for 20.2 miles, then turn right (north) onto Lake Crescent Road. After 0.1 mile, turn

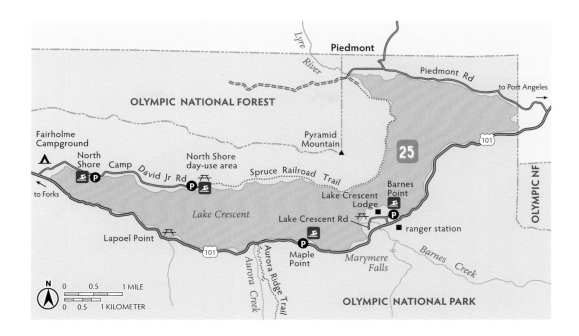

left to stay on Lake Crescent Road. After 0.3 mile, take a slight right to arrive at Lake Crescent Lodge and Log Cabin Resort; park and walk the 0.5-mile Moment in Time Trail (elevation gain: negligible; high point: 600 feet).

When you consider going to Lake Crescent, you might assume that it is going to be some kind of nightmare tourist situation. But you would be wrong. Yes, there are tourists, and of course the closer you get to Lake Crescent Lodge, the more populated the lake's beaches are. That's not surprising, as there are lots of reasons for lots of different types of folks to visit: nearby hikes such as the Marymere Falls, Aurora Ridge, Spruce Railroad, and Pyramid Mountain trails; easy access to favorite Olympic Peninsula towns Port Angeles (with its fabulous skate park) and Sequim (where you can visit the Manis Mastodon site, featuring the oldest remains of a mastodon in the Americas); the little Fairholme Store and Campground; fishing and kayaking and boating; and the surrounding tree-tastic Olympic National Park mountains. And yet, even at the height of summer on a perfect and glorious August day, there will be plenty of wiggle room. Even if it was more crowded, it would be totally worth it.

The water of Lake Crescent is stunning. Repeat: stunning. From the road it's bluer than blue, and when you get to the shore you find it a nuanced, almost tropical aqua. According to the National Park Service, this lake is low in nitrogen, so the usual phytoplankton are

So much to explore around Lake Crescent

noticeably absent. Looking at the lake, you might be confused for a second, thinking, "Am I in the Caribbean?" But no, it's straight-up Pacific Northwest.

It's beautiful year-round, though except for high summer in July and August, you'd have to prepare yourself for warming up after a polar plunge. And it's gorgeous and accessible from all angles—driving along the lakeshore from the east beach all the way to the northwest end, there are a number of fantastic access points, each special in its own way. Basically, you can pick your own adventure.

The swim featured here starts from Lake Crescent Lodge, with a short wooded walk on the Moment in Time Trail to a rocky beach with its shallow entry into the water. It has that rain-foresty feel and is great for the kids.

Or you could drive approximately 2 miles west of the lodge on US Highway 101 and look for an unmarked pullout on the right near Maple Point, identifiable by a little gap in the roadside barrier. You'll quickly forget your proximity to the highway when you get in the water and see that legendary deep blue depth just a few feet offshore, where there is an amazingly sharp drop-off, Washington's version of Dean's Blue Hole. If you want to free dive (and don't mind the less-than-tropical temperatures), this would be the spot to do it.

Another option is to turn off of US 101 at the west end, at Fairholme, and drive around the northwest shore on Camp David Jr. Road. If you're up for a somewhat treacherous traverse of a hillside strewn with fallen trees, park at the first pullout along this road and climb down. There might be a couple janky rope swings still hanging above shore (per usual, check before jumping). Smarter folks find this spot via kayak or canoe, which can be rented at Lake Crescent Lodge.

Approximately 1.5 miles farther down Camp David Jr. Road is the North Shore Day-Use Area, with picnic tables, a grill, and a dock. At the end of the dock—which has convenient boat ties—you get a panoramic view of the lake and the Olympic Mountains, plus plenty of height for taking a running leap into that stunning water.

Bring all the toys! (Swim #28)

GREATER SEATTLE AREA

AN ENTIRE GUIDEBOOK COULD be dedicated to the greater Seattle area. There are just so many places to get in the water, from Lake Washington to man-made Green Lake to Lake Union to salty Puget Sound. There are kid-friendly beaches and nudist-friendly beaches, places to launch stand-up paddleboards and kayaks and floaties, small public beaches hidden between homes, and docks jutting out into the water where urban anglers and techie sun worshippers haggle over space. No matter where you go, you're not too far from breweries and restaurants and the many thousands of people who call this metropolitan area home. On a good day, when there aren't many boats on the water, you might be able to find some quiet once you swim down into the dark water.

 ## PUGET SOUND: NORMANDY BEACH

TYPE: Sea-level saltwater
LOCATION: Roadside in Burien via I-5, SR 509, and SR 518
WATER: Very cold, clear, very dark blue
SEASON: April through September
WHO'S HERE: Kid-friendly, dog-friendly; locals mostly, fisherfolk, crabbers, paddleboarders, picnickers
AMENITIES: Food nearby
LOCAL'S TIP: The residents in the upscale community of Normandy Park really care about their beach, so be respectful.
GPS COORDINATES: 47.4503 N, –122.3789 W

GETTING THERE

From I-5, take exit 154B onto State Route 518 west toward Burien and the city of SeaTac. Stay straight as the highway becomes SW 148th Street. Turn left on Fourth Avenue SW, which turns into Sylvester Road SW. Turn right on SW 172nd Street and follow it to the corner of Maplewild Avenue SW. (Or, take SR 509 south to SE 160th Street, then turn left onto Sylvester Road SW. Turn right onto SW 172nd Street, and follow it to the corner of Maplewild Avenue SW.) Find limited street parking here.

BY BUS: From the Burien Transit Center, take Route 123/Gregory Heights to 14th Avenue SW and SW 160th Street, then walk 1.8 miles: Head south on 14th Avenue SW. After 0.2 mile, turn right onto SW 164th Street. Follow it for 0.4 mile, turn left onto 21st Avenue SW, then immediately bear right onto Marine View Drive SW. After 0.4 mile, the road name changes to 28th Avenue SW. Follow it for 0.1 mile, bear right onto SW 170th Street, then go 0.3 mile and turn left onto 33rd Avenue SW. After 400 feet, turn right onto unpaved Indian Trail. After 0.2 mile, arrive at SW 172nd Street.

BY BIKE: From the Burien Transit Center, take Route 123/Gregory Heights to 14th Avenue SW and SW 160th Street, then bike 2 miles: Head south on 14th Avenue SW. After 0.2 mile, turn right onto SW 164th Street. Follow it for 0.4 mile, turn left onto 21st Avenue SW, then immediately bear right onto Marine View Drive SW. After 0.4 miles, the road name changes to 28th Avenue SW. Follow it for 0.1 mile, then bear right onto SW 170th Street, then go 0.3 mile and veer right onto 33rd Avenue SW. After 0.2 mile, turn left onto Maplewild Avenue SW and in 0.4 mile arrive at SW 172nd Street.

If you are looking for a saltwater spot where you can get away from the hubbub without going too far from the city, Normandy Beach is the place for you. The portion open to the public is just a swath between private properties, so the beach is generally clean, quiet, and cared for. Normandy Beach is a bit unknown. It's surrounded by the homes of obviously well-organized people who are proud of their neighborhood, so go to Normandy only if you can adhere to general guidelines of etiquette and decency. Meaning: no garbage, no loud music, party only if you can do it discreetly. It's best for a relaxing, quiet day.

From the street parking, the quiet neighborhood beach is on the other side of a concrete barrier. The beach is a nice sun-exposed slope of small, smooth rocks and pebbles. Southern exposure keeps things generally warm, but there is no shade, so bring a towel for cushioning and an umbrella if you think you'll need a break from the sun. Bring a book and your paddleboard. Dogs are welcome and it's generally calm enough for kids.

The best thing about Normandy Beach is that you get the saltwater experience—Puget Sound is chock-full of crab and funny egg-shaped jellyfish—but it is enclosed enough by the surrounding landmasses that you don't have to worry about big waves or Jaws.

Finding a watery paradise within the urban boundaries

LAKE WASHINGTON: DENNY BLAINE BEACH

TYPE: Lowland lake, beach
LOCATION: Roadside in city park on east side of Capitol Hill in Seattle via Lake Washington Boulevard
WATER: Cold to warm, clearish, cleanish, blue-green
SEASON: Year-round
WHO'S HERE: Hipsters, families; topless women and naked men not uncommon; crowded, with a little bit of everyone; booze cruising and newly legalized joint passing; boaters farther out in the lake
AMENITIES: Portable toilet June through September; food nearby
LOCAL'S TIP: On busy days, park on 39th Avenue East, just south of Lake Washington Boulevard, and walk down to Denny Blaine through Viretta Park, adjacent to Kurt Cobain's old house.
GPS COORDINATES: 47.6201 N, –122.2806 W

GETTING THERE

From Lake Washington Boulevard at East Madison Street in Seattle, follow Lake Washington Boulevard south as it winds down to the lakeshore. Just past 39th Avenue East, turn left into a roundabout that marks Denny Blaine Beach at 200 Lake Washington Boulevard East. Park in the roundabout (limited number of spots) or find other street parking nearby. **BY BUS:** Take Route 2 from downtown Seattle to Madrona Drive and 38th Avenue East, then walk about 0.6 mile north along Lake Washington Boulevard and turn right at 200 Lake Washington Boulevard East. **BY BIKE:** Lake Washington Boulevard is a very popular bike route; on a number of summer Sundays, the street is closed to vehicle traffic south of Leschi, so combining a bike ride along this boulevard with a swim at Denny Blaine Beach makes for a great day of activity and refreshment. From anywhere on the boulevard, bike to 200 Lake Washington Boulevard East and turn east down to the lake.

Denny Blaine Beach is also known as Dykiki, referring to the popularity of this park with the LGBTQ community (note: creeps and Peeping Toms will not be tolerated). Its friendly nature and proximity to Capitol Hill make this beach a popular destination for city dwellers looking to soak up a bit of sun on summer days. As with most city beaches, it is most popular on weekends and sunny afternoons, so you can often enjoy this beach with minimal crowds earlier in the day or on cloudy days. June through September is the main season, but it's a great year-round spot for die-hard swimmers.

Denny Blaine Beach features a mostly grassy park area fronting the water, with a very small sandy beach. Small pebbles line the water's edge, with nice sand once you wade beyond knee deep. During peak season, this spot offers a good mix of sun and shade, but due to its eastern exposure, it loses sun early—about 6:00 p.m.—even in July and August.

Before the milfoil (a seaweed-like lake plant) and boat traffic get going in the summer, the water is quite nice and clean. Later in the summer, the milfoil tickles your belly a bit until you reach the deeper water, about 50 feet offshore. Families will enjoy the marked swimming area, shallow wading access, and ice-cream trucks that make regular laps all summer. On summer evenings and weekends, beware: there is lots of pot smoking and casual drinking on inflatables.

It's a nice swim out to the boating speed buoy, which most boats respect and stay away from. For longer swims, turn north or south beyond the privacy fences and swim along all

On a foggy day you can have Denny Blaine all to yourself.

the lakefront houses; stay close to the docks to avoid the boat traffic, and consider wearing a high-visibility swim cap or trailing a high-visibility float.

Denny Blaine is our favorite wintertime polar-plunge beach. We've developed a Sunday-morning ritual, meeting here at 9:00 a.m. to start the day: better than coffee . . . well, almost.

SNOQUALMIE RIVER: MCCORMICK PARK

TYPE: Lowland river, lazy current in summer, beach
LOCATION: Roadside in city park in Duvall east of Redmond via SR 520 and SR 203
WATER: Cool to warm, clearish, cleanish, blue-green
SEASON: June through September
WHO'S HERE: Kid-friendly, dog-friendly; families barbecuing, kids playing, people visiting local farms, cyclists
AMENITIES: Parking, restrooms, outdoor beach shower, picnic tables, grills; food nearby
LOCAL'S TIP: For six weeks during the summer, McCormick Park hosts a free Wednesday concert series; come for the swim, stay for the music.
GPS COORDINATES: 47.7406 N, −121.9891 W

GETTING THERE

From Redmond, east of I-405 via State Route 520, take Avondale Road NE to NE Novelty Hill Road and turn right onto it. After 0.7 mile, at a roundabout, take the second exit. After 4 miles, turn left onto West Snoqualmie Valley Road NE. After 0.3 mile, turn right onto NE 124th Street. After 1 mile, at a roundabout, take the third exit, onto SR 203/Carnation-Duvall Road NE. After 2.2 miles, turn left at unpaved NE Stephens Street and park in the lot.

This is a swimming hole for you loving parents and your lovely offspring. McCormick Park is a well-kept family spot, with easy access to all the amenities that make for a low-hassle day away that's lots of fun. It's definitely not somewhere you go to get away from it all, but it's the perfect place for a picnic and a swim. In short, this spot is excellent for a day trip with a swim as the central activity—or a supplement to the range of goings-on in the region.

Kids love the park's soft, sandy beach—there's a healthy 30-degree slope to it, great for rolling downhill or running around, without caretakers having to worry about little ones tripping over a boulder or taking a spill on some treacherous rocks. And it's wide open, too, providing a low-key view and ample sun all day long and then into the summertime evening. The water runs slow and cool; during the summer, the current is lazy, just right for relaxing on an inner tube under the big blue sky.

About 0.25 mile up from the main spot is Taylor Landing, which has a boat launch. This park isn't quite as pretty, but it is a little more private and slightly less civilized. When the water is low enough, you can walk from one park to the other.

We've included McCormick Park not only because it's a nice place to swim, but also because it's close to the quaint, epitomously Pacific Northwesty logging town of Duvall and other outdoorsy activities. Close at hand, you'll also find a dog park, a skate park, and many kid-friendly restaurants. Nearby farms are dedicated to organic and sustainable agriculture, and Sno-Valley Tilth provides farm tours throughout the summer and early fall. The Snoqualmie Valley Regional Trail runs through McCormick Park, winding 31.5 miles past the Snoqualmie Valley's lush farmlands from Carnation, Fall City, and Snoqualmie to North Bend. All kinds of folks use this trail: horseback riders, hikers, mountain bikers, birders, and good ol' regular walkers—before or after a swim.

Tube life

Dive into one of the many great spots in the Snoqualmie Pass region. (Swim #31)

SNOQUALMIE PASS AREA (AND WAY EAST)

INTERSTATE 90 ORIGINATES IN SEATTLE (at I-5) and continues east for more than 3000 miles. It crosses the Cascades at Snoqualmie Pass, which technically runs from North Bend and the Snoqualmie River in the west to Ellensburg and the Cle Elum River in the east.

There are an incredible number of opportunities for outdoor recreation in this area, which lies mostly within Mount Baker–Snoqualmie National Forest—including swimming in the many lakes and rivers. In fact, one of the nearby wilderness areas is named Alpine Lakes, stretching from Snoqualmie Pass nearly to Stevens Pass on US Highway 2. Farther east on I-90—across the Cascades and the Columbia River—is this book's far-eastern Washington swim, on the Palouse River north of Walla Walla.

 ## 29 MIDDLE FORK SNOQUALMIE RIVER: BLUE HOLE

TYPE: Lowland river, deep pool
LOCATION: Short walk on outskirts of North Bend via I-90 and SR 202
WATER: Cold to cool, clear, clean, blue-green
SEASON: Summer into fall
WHO'S HERE: Kid-friendly, dog-friendly; locals
AMENITIES: Food and lodging nearby
LOCAL'S TIP: Go to North Bend Bar and Grill for some homemade potato chips and to Pro Ski and Mountain Service for your hiking and camping needs.
GPS COORDINATES: 47.4976 N, −121.7643 W

You know the feeling—getting in that last swim as the sun goes down for the day.

GETTING THERE

From I-90 east of Seattle, take exit 31 onto State Route 202 north and follow it into North Bend. Turn right on First Street/East North Bend Way and turn left on Ballarat Avenue North. Turn right on NE Sixth Street and continue on it as it becomes SE 114th Street. Follow it to its end and park in the lot.

Locals call this little secret "Blue Hole." Out of all the swimming holes in this book, this is probably the most top-secret, which is interesting because it's really not the most unusual. Still, it's quite nice, a superdeep spot in the Middle Fork Snoqualmie River. Its location just on the outskirts of North Bend makes for very easy access, right off a nameless bike path–walking trail. There are small rapids upstream, so don't get in the water at higher flows.

From the parking lot at the end of the street, walk up onto a levee, then downriver 100 yards or so. Once you get to a bench beside a pine tree, you're there. That shoreline—river left—is pretty nondescript. Wading in, the water gets deep fast, so it's not great for kids or hesitant dogs.

Blue Hole is big enough to swim up and down and side to side—you can truly swim around in it, like being in a swimming pool—and it's deep enough that you may never see the bottom, even if you bring goggles and dive down deep. You could bring your stand-up paddleboard for some easy SUPing or an inflatable raft for lounging midriver.

Swim across to the river-right side for the rock feature, a small sloping cliff—it's not big enough for cliff jumping, but you can stand at water level and jump or dive in. If you like sunshine, you'll have to commit to swimming over to the river-right side, at least in the afternoon. Get all sweaty on nearby hikes up Mount Si, Little Si, Mailbox Peak, or Rattlesnake Ridge, then stop by here to cool off.

 ## SOUTH FORK SNOQUALMIE RIVER: THE DAM

TYPE: Lowland-forest river, current, pools, cliff jump
LOCATION: Roadside adjacent to Olallie State Park east of North Bend via I-90
WATER: Cold, clear, clean, blue-green
SEASON: Summer and fall
WHO'S HERE: Sunburned people, hikers, rock climbers, a good mix of all kinds
AMENITIES: Food and lodging nearby
LOCAL'S TIP: It's right off I-90, so take a dip here after your hike, before you go to your friend's barbecue back in town so everyone won't think you're a stinky hippie.
GPS COORDINATES: 47.4329 N, −121.6470 W

GETTING THERE

FROM I-90 EASTBOUND: From North Bend, take exit 38 west and at the end of the exit ramp, turn right onto SE Homestead Valley Road; after 1.3 miles, park along the south side of the road. **FROM I-90 WESTBOUND:** From Snoqualmie Pass, take exit 38 east and at the end of the exit ramp, turn left to go under the freeway and turn right onto SE Homestead Valley Road; after 1.3 miles, park along the south side of the road.

This tucked-away spot is right off the road. There's no fancy parking lot, though the road shoulder has plenty of room for several cars. No parking pass is needed. The 253-mile John Wayne Pioneer Trail has an access point nearby at the South Fork Picnic Area, so if you're a hard-core mountain biker who's had just about enough of sore buns and bugs in your teeth for the day, make this swim a quick drop-by on your long route. In fact, anyone could consider this place a drop-by, since the dam and the road are so close to the interstate. The place has an industrial feel, but even though it's not the most rustic swim spot of all time, it sure is pretty.

A personal bathtub for you on the South Fork Snoqualmie River

In addition to the inherent risk that comes with being in water, there is another safety item that must be addressed here: you're literally below a dam, and water can be released unexpectedly. During the prime swimming season (low water), the risk is low, but per usual, be careful and pay attention!

After parking, dart across the road and hop over the guardrail just downstream of the dam. It's a short 30-foot scramble down to the water's edge. Once you're in the river, you'll be hanging onto mostly bedrock granite. It's not just a bunch of measly rocks—it's a big slab, with little pools and current running around and over it. You can slide down or jump off the rock into the main pool; there's a little jump, around 3 to 5 feet high, and a bigger jump, upward of 10 feet. As you know, making jumps, no matter how small or big, is not 100 percent safe, so be careful.

The main activities here are swimming and hanging out on the rock. Once you're cooled off, take any of the many natural paths to find your way out of the water, or pull yourself out with the rope that is hanging down the side of the rock—another unique and fun feature of this spot—then walk back up to the road.

 ## 31 SOUTH FORK SNOQUALMIE RIVER: EXIT 38

TYPE: Lowland-forest river, current, beach
LOCATION: Short walk in Olallie State Park east of North Bend via I-90
WATER: Cold to cool, clear, clean, blue-green.
SEASON: Summer into early fall
WHO'S HERE: Kid-friendly, dog-friendly; bikers, hikers, climbers, teens with colorful t-shirts, families
AMENITIES: Parking, restrooms, rope swings; food and lodging nearby
NOTE: Day-use fee or Discover Pass required
LOCAL'S TIP: Climbers, check out the Far Side area, which includes five different crags (Overhaul, Gritstone, Gun Show, Interstate Park, and Winter Block); visit the Mountain Project website for more information (see Resources). Mountain bikers, check out a long, all-levels downhill ride off exit 38, given 3.2 hot peppers by a mountain biking website.
GPS COORDINATES: 47.4309 W, –121.6322 N

GETTING THERE

FROM I-90 EASTBOUND: From North Bend, take exit 38 west. Turn right and follow SE Homestead Valley Road for about 2 miles, then turn left under the freeway rather than taking the onramp back onto I-90. Park at the Far Side trailhead in Olallie State Park. FROM I-90 WESTBOUND: From Snoqualmie Pass, take exit 38 east. Turn right and park at the Far Side trailhead in Olallie State Park.

Don't let the unsexy name of this swimming hole turn you off. Yes, it happens to be just a hop, skip, and jump off Interstate 90, and yes, you can hear the cars speeding by in the near distance. But this noise mingles musically with the babbling brook and birdsong, and the proximity to civilization makes this spot ideal for a spontaneous swim. With so many climbing spots, bike routes, and hiking trails around, Exit 38 is another swimming hole perfect for a drop-by. When the water level is low and the current is slow, it's a fine place to bring kids, with a beach near picnic areas—as good as you can get, river-wise.

Swing into Exit 38, right off Interstate 90.

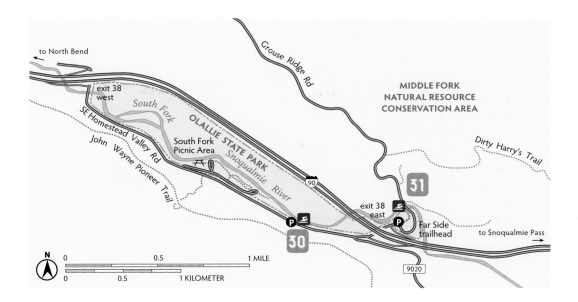

From the trailhead, it's a 0.1-mile shady, green walk on Dirty Harry's Trail. You'll be far enough away from your car that, for you die-hard urbanites, you'll feel like you're getting a break from the city and a little taste of ruggedness, but not so far away that you can't easily go back to get your left-behind cooler or use the restroom.

After a short jaunt down some rocks (this is the only part that may put older folk and little kids to the test), you arrive at a three-quarters-of-a-circle swath of medium-sand beach. The sun shines brightly here, providing an area to warm up post-swim. Despite its accessibility, the beach is generally very tidy, especially in the early summer. However, later in the season when this turns into more of a picnic spot, it's likely that signs of human activity will be more evident. In case of beach overpopulation, some river wading will take you to a wide, flat island. The sand here is a little chunkier, but you'll be surrounded on both sides by the river's flow.

The water is a lovely clear moss-green, and you can see small fish down below. If you swim perpendicular to the current, you'll get to a short wall of natural rock across from the beach—it's more of a shady perch than a jumping-off point. Just north is a bridge, and Instagram tells us that people do occasionally jump off of it, but we aren't certain about the water being an appropriate depth, so we don't recommend it (safety first, people, safety first!). Fortunately, if you are jonesing for that splash, on the underside of the bridge are two wee rinky-dink rope swings. A little swing gets you to the deeper part of the river without much to-do. Ponder the graffiti under the bridge, which says, "Takin' the Plunge."

32 MASON LAKE

TYPE: Mountain-forest lake, beach
LOCATION: Hike-in in Alpine Lakes Wilderness east of North Bend via I-90
WATER: Cold, clear, clean, blue-green
SEASON: June through September
WHO'S HERE: Kid-friendly, dog-friendly; medium-level hikers, backcountry campers
AMENITIES: Parking, outhouse, backcountry camping; other camping nearby
NOTES: Northwest Forest Pass required; wilderness permit required for backcountry camping
LOCAL'S TIP: If you want to continue on the hike, follow the main trail to the left around Mason Lake to the sign for Mount Defiance. It's another 1.7 miles to the summit.
GPS COORDINATES: 47.4249 N, –121.5833 W

GETTING THERE

FROM I-90 EASTBOUND: From North Bend, take exit 45 at Bandera and turn left to cross under the freeway. **FROM I-90 WESTBOUND:** From Snoqualmie Pass, take exit 45 at Bandera and turn right. **FROM EITHER APPROACH:** Veer left onto Forest Road 9030. After a little less than 1 mile, stay left at the fork onto FR 9031/ Mason Lake Road. At the end of this road, 3.8 miles from the freeway, park in the lot for the Ira Spring trailhead. Follow the Ira Spring Trail 3.4 miles (elevation gain: 2420 feet; high point: 4320 feet).

About an hour's drive from the greater Seattle area, Mason Lake can be either a half-day hike or a backcountry camping destination. Come early—this is a popular hike. It can get a little muddy near the lake, so leave your favorite suede Top-Siders at home. If you want to camp in the backcountry, get a free overnight wilderness permit at the trailhead.

The gravel parking lot has a fair number of parking spots, but as early morning turns into midmorning and the spots fill up, people tend to park on the side of the road. If you arrive late, be satisfied with parking behind the car in front of you—there's no rock-star parking here, because the road is wide enough for only one car. If you try to get closer, you might meet some cars trying to exit and end up having to back out all the way.

The Ira Spring Trail starts off easy. Initially it's soft and flat, which your knees will surely appreciate on the way back down, and wide enough to walk three abreast. At 0.8 mile, you come to a bridge over a waterfall on Mason Creek, where the grade starts to pick up, and soon you cross into the Alpine Lakes Wilderness. From here, this hike becomes fairly steep. You walk under birch trees, with occasional gaps overhead that let in the sun. Every opportunity for open viewing is worth taking, so pause to check out the forests in the distance. Starting at 1.6 miles, there's a 1.3-mile stretch where you have to walk over and around good-size rocks.

Once you get above the tree line, some switchbacks lead up, to the top of a ridge at 2.9 miles. You might miss the view from here on the way up since it will be behind you to the south, but on the way down, it is impossible to ignore: Mount Rainer in the distance, but from a vantage point that's more on the same level as the massive mountain than the one we're used to from the lowlands. It's really quite stunning. Near the top of the ridge, the trail to the right traverses along Bandera Mountain, but stay left to reach Mason Lake.

After the crest, it's about 0.5 mile down through, to quote a friend, "a gosh-darn wonderland." There is much shade from the fir trees, a nice break after the sun- and wind-exposed climb you've just accomplished. Be prepared to climb over or under a couple fallen logs. There's a little waterfall with large stepping-stones to navigate at the beginning of the clearing. And then: many choices.

The water at Mason Lake is almost too pretty to swim in.

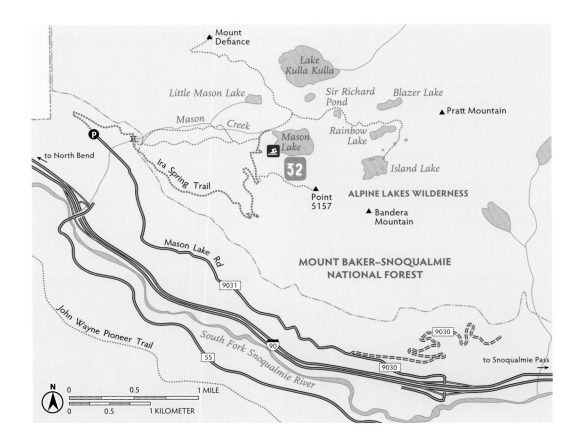

Mason Lake has an abundance of entry points, so take your time choosing. You can walk around the lake to get a better sense of the options, or spend a night (or two or three) and try them all. If you like a sandy, shallow wade-in, you're in luck; if you prefer getting in via a big smooth boulder, you have lots of those to choose from, too. There's even a patch with a strange, lovely green sand, with a bit of a drop-off a few yards out.

The few campsites are first-come, first-served. Camp so that you can get the dusky sunset swim after the day hikers leave, as well as that quiet early-morning swim before the next day's hikers arrive. Trout love this lake too, so you might see some anglers. You can also hike past Mason Lake to Rainbow Lake, Island Lake, and beyond.

33 MIRROR LAKE

TYPE: Subalpine lake, cliff jump, beach
LOCATION: Hike-in in Okanogan–Wenatchee National Forest south of Snoqualmie Pass via I-90 and FR 54
WATER: Cold to cool, clear, clean, blue-green
SEASON: Late spring through early fall
WHO'S HERE: Kid-friendly, dog-friendly; recreationists, hikers, families, Boy and Girl Scout groups, backcountry campers
AMENITIES: Backcountry camping; food and lodging nearby at Snoqualmie Pass
NOTES: Northwest Forest Pass required; wilderness permit required for backcountry camping
LOCAL'S TIP: Much more well-known and popular Snow Lake is 20 miles away. Go to Mirror Lake instead—for every 200 people at Snow Lake, you'll find 20 here.
GPS COORDINATES: 47.3441 N, –121.4246 W

GETTING THERE

From I-90 east of Snoqualmie Pass, take exit 62 for Stampede Pass and Kachess Lake. At the stop sign, turn west onto Forest Road 54. After approximately 0.5 mile, cross a bridge over the Yakima River. Drive for 0.6 mile, then turn right onto gravel FR 5480. Watch out for bikers and hikers, since the road parallels the Iron Horse Trail. After 4.2 miles, go straight on the middle road to continue on FR 5480 past Lost Lake. After 6.1 miles, park in the lot at the sign for Mirror Lake. Hike the 2.3-mile trail (elevation gain: 870 feet; high point: 4200 feet).

The Cascade Range divides Washington into two sections: the wetter, more-temperate side to the west and the drier, more continental-climate side to the east. Going even just a couple miles east of Snoqualmie Pass gets you into sunshine territory. Mirror Lake, while barely east of the pass, is within that drier (and warmer in summer) environment.

Park at the lower parking lot. If you have four-wheel drive you can keep driving to an upper parking lot, which skips about 0.5 mile of trail walking. Four-wheel drive can come in handy at the lower parking lot, as well, since there's not much room or space for overflow parking, so you might have to get creative on a busy weekend.

Take the path up a rocky hill to the trailhead, roughly 0.5 mile. Keep an eye out, because there is no official signage—instead, the trailhead is at a wooden marker and possibly some cairns. This trail takes you in a downward direction (if you head uphill, you're going to find a good view but no lake). In another 0.5 mile or so, you'll pass smaller and marshier little

Textbook cliff jump entry form

Cottonwood Lake, and you may choose to hang out or even camp here for a bit more solitude. In total, the hike is an easy 2.3 miles, with a nice mix of trail conditions from buffed-out soft forest duff to some rockier sections that require you to pay attention to your footing. When you reach Mirror Lake, you'll see that a trail loops almost all the way around it.

The more traveled section, to the left, is the Pacific Crest Trail, which goes clockwise about a third of the way around the lake before continuing on to Yakima Pass and, eventually, all the way to Mexico. There are many access points along that route, and where the PCT leaves the lakeshore to continue south, there's a short lakeshore trail to a beach and some nice backcountry campsites. If you set up there, plan to share the space or the sites with others. Beyond this spur trail, the southwest lakeshore has sketchier traveling, so it might not be possible to complete a loop around the lake.

Back at where the Mirror Lake Trail reaches Mirror Lake at its junction with the PCT, go to the right, or counterclockwise, to get to some cliff jumping, at about a quarter of the way around the lake. The water below you is gorgeous, blue, and clear. The cliff is not at straight vertical and requires a jump out, but it's not difficult and only 10 or 15 feet above very deep water. There's also a big log to jump off of. Other places in this section of shoreline have more ramp-style access points, as well as a few smaller campsites.

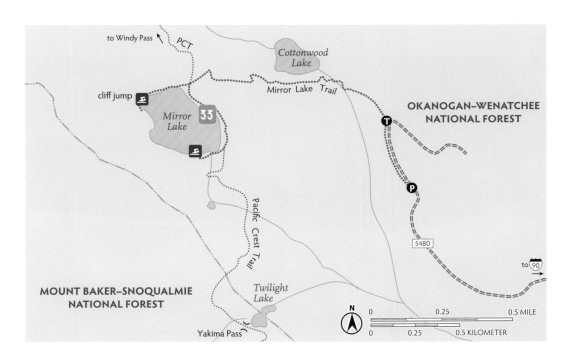

You can go beyond Mirror Lake by taking the PCT north for about 3 miles to Windy Pass, on the back side of the Summit at Snoqualmie ski area (this is also an alternate trailhead for the hike to Mirror Lake).

34 CLE ELUM RIVER: AT SALMON LA SAC

TYPE: Mountain-forest river, small rapids and eddies, current, pools
LOCATION: Roadside in Okanogan–Wenatchee National Forest northwest of Cle Elum via I-90 and SR 903
WATER: Cold to cool, clear, clean, blue-green
SEASON: Late June until rains start
WHO'S HERE: Kid-friendly, dog-friendly; families, teenagers, recreationists, hikers, tubers, campers, RVers, ATVers
AMENITIES: Camping, food, and lodging nearby
NOTE: Northwest Forest Pass required
LOCAL'S TIP: On the way in or out, check out Roslyn. The town's claim to fame: the site of filming for the critically acclaimed early-1990s show *Northern Exposure*.
GPS COORDINATES: 47.3834 N, −121.0963 W

Floating through the little rapid on Cle Elum River

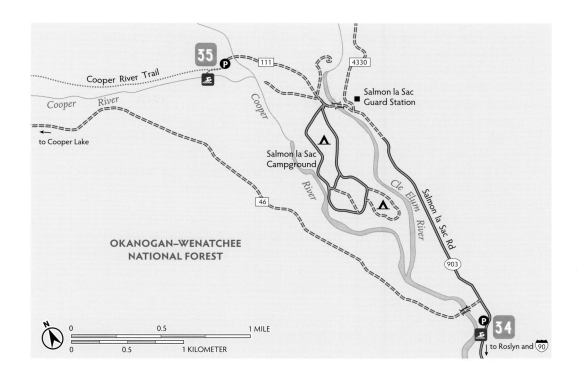

GETTING THERE

From I-90 east of Snoqualmie Pass, take exit 80 for Roslyn and Salmon la Sac. Turn left onto Bullfrog Road and go 2.1 miles. At the traffic circle, take the first exit, which continues on Bullfrog Road. In another 0.7 mile, at the next traffic circle, continue straight onto State Route 903 north, and go 1.5 miles. Turn left onto West Nevada Avenue to stay on SR 903. Drive 14 miles until you see a small parking area on the left side of the road just before Forest Road 46.

Just upstream of the town of Roslyn, Salmon la Sac is not a designated town—rather, it's an area that has never quite made it to city status but has long been in use. Today, people come to this point on the Cle Elum River for some really excellent tubing, swimming, and floating under a sunny blue sky. Since it's east of the Cascade crest, it'll likely be sunny and warm over here during the June gloom season of the Puget Sound area. But the river could still be high in June—except during drought years—so aim for late June or later. This isn't a party crowd—for more of a scene, head to the Cooper River cliff jump (Swim #35).

Right off State Route 903, downstream from where the Cooper River flows into the Cle Elum River, pull over and park, then walk 100 feet west to the water's edge. Here a big rock abuts the river. At the point where it juts out into the water, it creates a very small whitewater rapid—at low flow, it's small enough to swim in without worrying about getting pulled under or pushed downstream.

On the downstream side of the rock is a big blue pool to jump into from the rock; down in the eddy below the rapid, you can swim against a little current or let it carry you downstream. On the upstream side of the rock, above the rapid, the rock drops down into a big shallow pool, which is protected by the rock and more accessible for kids—like a big natural kiddie pool. Sitting in the middle of the river is another big rock, which you can swim to and then hang out on with the water flowing past you on either side. Check out the other side of this middle rock, toward river right, for another big pool. This one is superclear since there's no whitewater.

Sitting on the rocky beach or on the rocks, you'll see all kinds of people in all kinds of watercrafts—cheap superstore rafts, duckies, inflatable canoes. Many of them launch from around the bridge upstream for a mellow ride. At low water, this stretch of the Cle Elum River is relatively safe to tube or float. But don't worry if you forgot your vessel—there are so many wonderful features to keep you occupied, and the swimming is so fun that you don't really need equipment.

The Salmon la Sac and Cayuse Horse campgrounds are north up SR 903 with sites in both sun and shade and a picnic area for day use. Many opportunities for hiking extend from this area—the Waptus River Trail, Cooper River Trail, and Red Mountain Trail, to name a few. These trails have access points to Waptus Lake, Cooper Lake, and Little Joe Lake, respectively.

 ## 35 COOPER RIVER CLIFF JUMP

TYPE: Mountain-forest river, cliff jump
LOCATION: Short walk in Okanogan–Wenatchee National Forest northwest of Cle Elum via I-90 and SR 903
WATER: Cold to cool, clear, clean, blue-green
SEASON: Summer into fall
WHO'S HERE: Dog-friendly; grownups, dogs, dudes, hikers, campers
AMENITIES: Parking, campground, outhouse
NOTE: Northwest Forest Pass required
LOCAL'S TIP: This spot is not the most family-friendly; go about 10 miles downstream to the Cle Elum River spot (Swim #34) for more-wholesome fun. And don't forget to clean up your trash!
GPS COORDINATES: 47.4092 N, –121.1081 W

Picture-perfect swimming hole

GETTING THERE

From I-90 east of Snoqualmie Pass, take exit 80 for Roslyn and Salmon la Sac. Turn left onto Bullfrog Road and go 2.1 miles. At the traffic circle, take the first exit, which continues on Bullfrog Road. In another 0.7 mile, at the next traffic circle, continue straight onto State Route 903 north, and go 1.5 miles. Turn left onto West Nevada Avenue to stay on SR 903. Drive for 15 miles, and when the pavement ends, continue straight on Salmon la Sac Road. The dirt roads for the last mile or so are usually well graded. In 0.2 mile, stay left to cross the bridge over the Cle Elum River and reach a Y junction near the Salmon la Sac Campground. Follow signs to the Cooper River Trail: veer right, to a three-way junction, and take the middle road, Forest Road 111. In 0.9 mile arrive at the well-established Cooper River trailhead, where there's plenty of parking. More parking is available at the nearby Salmon la Sac Campground.

The Cooper River cliff jump is a mecca for outdoor enthusiasts. This is where all kinds of active folk converge: hikers dropping by from the popular Cooper River Trail; kayakers passing through, then taking out their kayaks downstream near the trailhead; campers walking over from the nearby Salmon la Sac Campground. And, of course, cliff jumpers.

Now, not to be sexist, but good cliff jumps tend to attract dudes, in the modern sense— fit young guys with a little more courage than common sense. Of course, in a future better world, cliff jumpers might have more equal representation, since everyone would have equally functional swimwear, and no one would have to worry about losing theirs midair. Last time we were there, a bachelor party was in celebration mode, which at least shows a little Pacific Northwest spirit, given that some alternatives are seedy compared to a day with the bros at the river.

It's just a short distance to the primary attraction, the cliff: walk 0.1 mile up the Cooper River Trail and then follow the beaten paths down to the rocky shoreline. The steep dirt slope between the Cooper River Trail and the water will be your exit point, and it is just tricky enough to make you hesitate if you were thinking about bringing your kids. Dogs, on the other hand, seem to have no problem entering and exiting the water at this point. In fact it's difficult to even get in the water here if you're not willing to take the 10-foot jump. The water itself is deep and beautiful, clear and calm once your splash settles. On the flat rocks above, you can sunbathe and listen to the bubbling patch of whitewater upstream and the river roaring by.

The 7.8-mile Cooper River Trail is famously kid-friendly, so if you have some juvenile hikers in your care, a flatter beach on shallower water is just a short way downstream, near the trailhead parking area. Bring along another caretaker, so that you can take turns babysitting and cliff hucking.

36 PALOUSE RIVER: PALOUSE FALLS STATE PARK

TYPE: Lowland river, waterfalls
LOCATION: Hike-in in state park east of Vantage via I-90, SR 26, and SR 261
WATER: Clear and cool, turns warmer and more algae-y in late August, blue-green
SEASON: Late spring through late summer
WHO'S HERE: Kid-friendly, leashed-dog–friendly; hikers, campers, picnickers
AMENITIES: Parking, restrooms, picnic tables, camping (first-come, first-served)
NOTES: Day-use fee or Discover Pass required; dogs must be leashed
LOCAL'S TIP: If you are headed toward Walla Walla via SR 261 and US 12, you pass through Starbuck, home of the Rawhide Saloon. You'll see some handwritten signs pointing the way on the lonely road from Palouse Falls. Stop! It is a biker-hiker-locals hangout with a feisty owner, surprisingly good food, and buckets of ice-cold beer. Plus pull tabs and horseshoes.
GPS COORDINATES: 46.6636 N, –118.2281 W

GETTING THERE

FROM I-90 AT THE COLUMBIA RIVER: On the east side of the Vantage bridge, take exit 137 to merge onto State Route 26 east toward Othello and Pullman; after 83 miles, reach the small town of Washtucna and turn right (south) onto Main Street. FROM I-90 AT RITZVILLE: Take exit 221 to SR 261 south and follow it 27 miles to Washtucna. FROM EITHER DIRECTION: Drive south through town on

Palouse Falls, Washington's official state waterfall (photo by alohadave/iStockphoto)

> SR 260/SR 261 for 6.4 miles and turn left onto SR 261 south. There are signs here for Palouse Falls State Park. Follow the highway for 8.5 miles and turn left onto Palouse Falls Road, clearly marked with a sign indicating "Palouse Falls State Park." Drive 2.4 miles and enter the state park; the last stretch turns to gravel as you drive to the road-end parking area. Hike the 0.5-mile trail (elevation loss: 200 feet; high point: 800 feet).

About an hour's drive from Walla Walla, Palouse Falls was named *Aput Aput*, or "Falling Water," by the Palouse Indians. Washington State's official waterfall is especially spectacular in late spring and early summer, when the water level is highest and clearest. Even from the state park's large parking lot, you can see the beautiful Palouse Falls and Palouse Lake. Some of the campsites have excellent views of the falls as well.

Most visitors are families out for the day, and if you stay close to the parking lot, you might find yourself among the many folks who stick to the picnic areas above the vista points. However, an easy hike takes you to a truly special destination: the Upper Falls swimming hole. It's far enough away from civilization to feel totally remote.

The trail to the Upper Falls is unmarked, but rangers, if present, will give you directions; otherwise, look for trails alongside the railroad tracks, which start on the far side of the parking lot where the restrooms are. As far as difficulty goes, a friend's six-year-old and ten-year-old handled this walk just fine, but there's a bit of scrambling over large rocks and loose gravel, so it may not be appropriate for everyone. Definitely not a flip-flop kind of trail—wear your walking shoes.

About five minutes into the 0.5-mile walk, the trail branches off and down along a fairly steep cliff that is exposed on one side. It's not difficult to navigate, but it can be a little intimidating at first glance. Continue alongside the railroad tracks for about 50 yards, and then down a hill of loose gravel. Upper Falls is at the bottom. Warning: Because of the algae (especially later in the season) and the very smooth rock, the entire area can be slippery, so be careful both when walking around the Upper Falls and when jumping in.

Upper Falls is a series of small waterfalls and gorgeous swimming holes above Palouse Falls. While it's upriver from the falls, it is safe to swim in—the water is very slow (especially late in the summer) and there's no real way that you could slip into the faster-moving river below Upper Falls. In later August, the water is cool but not icy—very refreshing on a hot day after the hike in. Regular hikers may make the journey in from the Palouse Falls vista area, but few swim, so the swimming hole itself is usually almost empty.

During the day, the Upper Falls are exposed to the sun, with plenty of great spots for sunbathing. For those who tend to get a little lobstery, there is a shady area at the cliff base.

The waterfalls are small enough that you can swim under them, and one even has a rock shelf right under the falls that is perfect to sit on.

You can jump into the water from medium-height rock outcroppings. The water is fairly clear, and it's mostly easy to gauge its depth, but there are some shallow, harder-to-see rocks, so definitely test the depth of any area before you jump. Above the Upper Falls, the Palouse River is interrupted by lots of rock formations and becomes a series of tributaries, perfect for kids to explore.

Will you walk the log at Big Eddy
(and jump)? (Swim #38)

STEVENS PASS AND LEAVENWORTH AREA

PART OF THE CASCADE LOOP Scenic Byway, US Highway 2 runs perpendicular to the Cascade Range, just as Snoqualmie Pass does to the south on Interstate 90. The Stevens Pass summit (and ski area) is approximately 83 miles east of the Puget Sound area, surrounded by forests: Mount Baker–Snoqualmie National Forest to the west, Okanogan–Wenatchee National Forest to the east. The Alpine Lakes Wilderness extends north from I-90 nearly to US 2, including the Icicle Creek area and the Stuart Range.

On the east side of Stevens Pass, Leavenworth is the big tourist attraction and one of Washington's true mountain towns. It has a (faux) Bavarian theme and annually hosts Octoberfest—bratwurst and lederhosen are available year-round. The Wenatchee River flows through it, down from Lake Wenatchee and White River.

The Wenatchee River has no single best swimming hole; rather, tons and tons of access points beckon to those willing to choose their own adventure. In fact, the whole river is good for swimming, and some spots are better or worse depending on what you're after. None of them are very far out of town—they're accessible rather than wildernessy—and all of the Wenatchee River swim spots in this chapter center around Leavenworth.

37 SKYKOMISH RIVER: AL BORLIN PARK

TYPE: Lowland river, beach
LOCATION: Short walk from city park or roadside in Monroe via US 2 and SR 203
WATER: Cold, clearish, cleanish, blue-green
SEASON: Summer through fall
WHO'S HERE: Kid-friendly, dog-friendly; everyone, lots of families
AMENITIES: Parking, restrooms, picnic tables; food nearby
LOCAL'S TIP: Bring your inner tube.
GPS COORDINATES: 47.8464 N, –121.9706 W

GETTING THERE

From US 2 in Monroe, head east toward Stevens Pass. Turn right on North Lewis Street, which becomes South Lewis Street after crossing Main Street and State Route 203 after crossing the Skykomish River. Just before the SR 203 bridge, turn left into the park and park in the large parking lot, or drive over the bridge and pull over to park on the shoulder.

Al Borlin Park is a gorgeous, secluded 90 acres of forested land near the quiet city of Monroe. Folks on the interwebs can't get enough of this little bridge over the water, the abandoned railroad track, and the beautiful backwoods trails, where they let Spot and Rex run off-leash in this serene small-town park. And then there's the beach: a long strip on either side of the Skykomish, where grandpappy, mama Sue, and lil' squirt can play in the curve of the river or relax on land.

From the big, easy-to-access, obvious parking lot on the north side of the river, walk about 0.25 mile alongside South Lewis Street and under the bridge to access the shore just downstream of the bridge, where the beach has a grainy-rock feel. The south side of the river has no official place to park but there's enough room to pull over off the road next to the sandy shore. You'll be surprised by how naturey the riverfront feels, with a mature forest above the riverbank and the traffic noise fading away once you get down to the beach. This is definitely a family-friendly spot—and it's also friendly to folks who like to get a little rowdy. Here, that's often one and the same (moms and dads need to let loose every now and then, too).

Many people come to Al Borlin Park beach for the inner tubing. Just take a walk about 0.5 mile or so upstream along park trails or the riverbank, then sit your derriere in your tube and enjoy the ride. Some people drive all the way up US Highway 2 to Sultan to tube down to this park, but be forewarned: that's a long ride. When we were last at Al Borlin, we saw a very bedraggled woman disembark from her tube. Seems that her friend had

All kinds of fun times at Al Borlin Park

misinformed her about the timeline of Sultan-to-Monroe tube travel, and she'd spent a little too long in the sun without proper provisions. If you decide to tube from upriver to here, plan ahead and check the weather and river conditions before doing so.

There's a public-pool type of vibe, but don't let that turn you off—the park stretches way upstream, with tons of trails to explore and lots of room to move around. If you're a latte kind of person and you find yourself caught in an Americano crowd, you can always relocate to a more ideal spot. If you're more of a wine drinker than a PBR person, Woodinville wine country is only a twenty-minute drive south via State Route 522. Disclaimer: Swim first, drink second; don't drink and swim. Also, don't drink and drive. And definitely don't drink and share your feelings on social media.

 ## 38 SKYKOMISH RIVER: BIG EDDY

TYPE: Lowland river, eddy, beach
LOCATION: Roadside in Mount Baker–Snoqualmie National Forest east of Gold Bar via US 2
WATER: Cold, clear, clean, blue-green
SEASON: Late summer through early fall
WHO'S HERE: Kid-friendly; weekdays—recreationists, fisherfolk, kayakers; weekends—everyone
AMENITIES: Parking, restrooms; food nearby
NOTE: Discover Pass required
LOCAL'S TIP: You can float downstream in an inner tube. Lazy good fun!
GPS COORDINATES: 47.8360 N, –121.6576 W

From US Highway 2 in the town of Gold Bar, head east on the highway 2 miles and cross over the Skykomish River Bridge. Park in the gravel lot on the right.

Big Eddy is just a couple miles from the town of Gold Bar and directly off US Highway 2, so it's easily accessible. This place is not a secret, nor a place for solitude, but it's high quality and fun. It's a social beach with lots of families and kids. On one visit we saw three full-size barbecue grills—not the little hibachi grills, mind you, but full-size backyard grills. However, car break-ins have been an issue in the past, so don't leave anything of value in your vehicle. And because valuable items are known to get lost in sand and water, plan accordingly before leaving home: don't bring more than you have to.

Big Eddy is pretty self-explanatory. It's a giant eddy, or calm pool, in this big river. However, eddies can have very strong river currents if the flow is even moderate, so it's important to swim only at the lowest flows. Luckily, Big Eddy is still quite big and deep during the Skykomish's low flows.

The access is just past the bridge, on the right. There's a mixed rocky, sandy beach that offers easy, moderately steep access into the pool. While you can find shade above the river shore, the area by the eddy is mostly in full sun; bring a sun tent if you need it. As of

Wade in or leap in.

I double-dog-dare you!

this writing, a pile of logs on the opposite shore had one big log sticking out over the flow, acting as a convenient diving board from which to jump off. Rocks and other logs that line the near shore are a great feature for some monkey play—but be mindful of conditions and aware of currents.

Steelhead, salmon, and trout call this river home, so swimmers share the beach with anglers, as well as boaters (only nonmotorized boats are allowed here). People bring kayaks, canoes, and rafts to launch for a two- or three-hour journey downriver (longer if just floating and not paddling) to the town of Sultan. This is a Class II ride, with some chop mostly in the first quarter mile.

39 LAKE WENATCHEE

TYPE: Lowland-forest lake, beach
LOCATION: Roadside in Okanogan–Wenatchee National Forest north of Leavenworth via US 2 and SR 207
WATER: Cold, clear, clean, blue-green
SEASON: Summer into fall
WHO'S HERE: Locals in the know
AMENITIES: Camping, food, and lodging nearby
LOCAL'S TIP: Stop at Coles Corner to fill up your tank and grab a bite.
GPS COORDINATES: 47.8217 N, –120.7570 W

GETTING THERE

From US Highway 2 at Stevens Pass, head east for 20 miles and turn left onto State Route 207 at a junction known as Coles Corner. After 5.3 miles, turn left onto County Road 22/North Shore Drive. After 1.1 miles, park on the roadside.

Lake Wenatchee is a big snowmelt- and glacial-fed lake located in Okanogan–Wenatchee National Forest on the eastern slope of the Cascades, near the towns of Leavenworth, Cashmere, and Wenatchee. It's 5 miles long and 244 feet deep at its deepest. This is a popular area for just about any outdoor activity you could think of: mountain biking, hiking, horseback riding, boating, fishing, rafting, golfing, birding, windsurfing, or camping. (Come in the winter for snowshoeing, cross-country skiing, and dogsledding.) Lake Wenatchee State Park has 155 campsites, and there are plenty of bed-and-breakfasts, cabins, and lodges to rent, as well as RV campgrounds. Stay for a day, a week, a month, and you'll still have tons to do and places to explore.

Of course, there are many obvious places to go swimming around the lake. To find an access point away from the locals and tourists, you can drive around the lakeshore, paying attention to private-property signs and no-parking signs as you go. This swim's particular

Finding the swimming hole through the trees

spot has no signage—you just pull over to the side of the road and then walk down a beaten trail for about 200 feet to the water.

There's a cobble and gravel beach, where you'll likely be secluded and not have to worry about your dog shaking off on someone else's towel or running across somebody's pizza. Since it's not a marked spot, expect to find only locals and yourself, dear reader. There's really not much to it—no cliffs, no dock, just space to lounge and take in the beauty of this Pacific Northwest environment. The water is fairly cold, but due to lots of sun exposure, it tends to warm up a bit during the summer. If you want to skip going into Leavenworth and dealing with the tourism scene, sneak in to this quiet little spot.

WHITE RIVER FALLS

TYPE: Mountain-forest river, current, waterfall, pool, beach
LOCATION: Roadside in Okanogan–Wenatchee National Forest northwest of Lake Wenatchee via US 2 and SR 207
WATER: Very cold, silty, clean, milky turquoise green
SEASON: Late summer
WHO'S HERE: Kid-friendly; recreationists, campers
AMENITIES: Parking, outhouse, picnic tables, campground
NOTE: Northwest Forest Pass required
LOCAL'S TIP: Check the road status. If there's a fire in the region, firefighting efforts can damage roads and make soil unstable, with higher chances of erosion, falling trees, or road washouts. If this happens, park farther down the road and walk the road to the campground.
GPS COORDINATES: 47.9525 N, –120.9397 W

GETTING THERE

From US 2 at Stevens Pass, drive east 20 miles to State Route 207. Turn left and drive 11 miles, passing Lake Wenatchee, then stay right on Forest Road 6400/White River Road. Drive 9 miles on FR 6400/White River Road and keep right into White River Falls Campground; park in the day-use area.

White River Falls is high up in the Cascades, the farthest out of Leavenworth in this chapter, which means it's away from crowds. In a way, this swimming hole just outside the Glacier Peak Wilderness is more about how photogenic it is rather than its having truly great swimming. Fed by glaciers on the flanks of Glacier Peak, the glacial meltwater is stunningly aqua blue, like a robin's egg, and more opaque than some rivers because it contains lots of silt and sediment. It's probably one of the coldest rivers in this book, and also one of the prettiest. If you can, visit this spot on the last days of summer or first warm fall days, when the season is starting to change in Wenatchee Valley, for some additional autumn colors in this already dazzling photo op.

You'd think, going by its name, that White River Falls would be a waterfall, but it's more like a cascade of a bunch of little waterfalls, rather than being a truly big waterfall. The last fall into the pool has a stronger hydraulic than you may think at first, especially to novice eyes, so be aware of the danger and don't swim under it or get too close, because the hydraulic could suck you in and be hard to get out of.

White River Falls is right by the White River Falls Campground, about 100 feet downstream from where you parked. The pool itself is surrounded by big cliffs, and as the river moves on downstream these cliffs morph into big rocks. From that point and down, you could launch a stand-up paddleboard or kayak, though you would deal with hazards such as rocks and current, so unless you're experienced, this might not be a safe option.

White River Falls is picture perfect.

It's like your own deserted island in Tumwater Canyon.

Upstream, at a big, log-jammed bend in the river, a sandy beach would be a better spot for families. At high water, the river breaks into two channels, and at low water it becomes one again with the overflow channel drying up. When this happens, the overflow channel becomes more like a series of pools connected by a little trickle, which is quite safe and fun for kids to splash about in.

The White River Falls Campground, situated beneath old-growth Douglas firs, has five campsites, but if it's full you can go to nearby Grasshopper Meadows or Napeequa Crossing campgrounds just downstream.

 41 WENATCHEE RIVER: TUMWATER CANYON

TYPE: Lowland-forest river, current, pool, beach
LOCATION: Roadside in Okanogan–Wenatchee National Forest just north of Leavenworth via US 2
WATER: Cold, clear, clean, blue-green
SEASON: Late summer into early fall
WHO'S HERE: Rock and ice climbers, recreationists, hikers, kayakers
AMENITIES: Parking; camping, food, and lodging nearby
NOTE: Northwest Forest Pass required
LOCAL'S TIP: In the spring, watch expert whitewater kayakers tackle this section, which is one of the highest-volume Class V rivers in the state.
GPS COORDINATES: 47.6070 N, –120.7167 W

GETTING THERE

FROM STEVENS PASS: Drive 31 miles on US Highway 2 eastbound toward Leavenworth. **FROM LEAVENWORTH:** Drive 3.6 miles on US 2 westbound toward Stevens Pass. **FROM EITHER DIRECTION:** Park on the north side of the highway in a giant pullout.

Tumwater Canyon—the Wenatchee River roughly from where US Highway 2 crosses the river in the north downstream to the city of Leavenworth—is popular for hiking, rock climbing, and kayaking. There are lots of pullouts along US 2 on the east side of the Cascades, making this highway perfect if you've spent a weekend in the mountains and want a quick swim as you're starting to head home.

This section of the river can have big whitewater rapids, especially when the water is running at full volume. During that time, this spot won't be good for swimming because (a) the beach will be underwater and (b) the current will be too strong. Even in low water, the rapids are fairly large, so this area is not safe for inner tubing or rafting. However, you can find pools that are calm, but always be aware of what's downstream and around the corner.

At this spot deep in Tumwater Canyon, pull over to the north side of the highway where the parking is less organized than farther downstream; it's more like a giant pullout. Be careful when crossing the highway—it's busy! After you cross the road, clamber over the guardrail to get to the sandy beach.

You can wade across shin-deep water to get to a sandy island. On the other side of the island is a giant pool: really big and really deep. Stand-up paddleboarders could do laps around the island without going downriver. There's a little current to play in but not so much that you'll get carried downstream. A very interesting and photogenic spot.

 WENATCHEE RIVER: POINT 76

TYPE: Lowland-forest river, current, pools, beach
LOCATION: Roadside just west of Leavenworth via US 2
WATER: Cold, clear, clean, blue-green
SEASON: Late summer
WHO'S HERE: Kid-friendly, dog-friendly; rock climbers, families, recreationists
AMENITIES: Parking, outhouse; food and lodging nearby
LOCAL'S TIP: Walk across the bridge and hike up or down the river-right trail to find your own personal beach.
GPS COORDINATES: 47.5871 N, –120.7075 W

A great spot in Tumwater Canyon, once the snowmelt subsides

GETTING THERE

FROM STEVENS PASS: Drive 32.1 miles on US Highway 2 eastbound toward Leavenworth. **FROM LEAVENWORTH:** Drive 2.5 miles on US 2 westbound toward Stevens Pass. **FROM EITHER DIRECTION:** Park in the parking lot (room for twenty cars) on the south side of the highway.

The Wenatchee River is a "drop-pool" river, meaning it has whitewater rapids interspersed with pools. These pools are quite deep, and you can fully swim in them and dive down into their blue depths. This spot is just one beach among many in this stretch of Tumwater Canyon, so you can scout out your own personal beach.

This section of the river can have big whitewater rapids, especially when the water is running at full volume. During that time, this spot won't be good for swimming because (a) the beaches will be underwater and (b) the current will be too strong. Even in low water, the rapids are fairly large, so this area is not safe for inner tubing or rafting. However, you can find pools that are calm; just always be aware of what's downstream and around the corner.

From the parking lot, head down the path leading directly to a nice beach, easily accessible and good for kids. This beach has no boulders and is flat, with a swath of sandy ground and deep pools. You can walk upriver to a bridge and cross to the other shoreline, which is also dotted with lots of other sandy beaches. It's simply a matter of how far you want to walk—you'll still be near the highway, but you can get a beach to yourself. Each of these beaches has more or less character, in terms of having boulders versus none and being steep versus flat, but they all share the traits of having sandy beaches and deep blue pools. If you get lucky with some heat in September, head over to this stretch of beach to catch some autumn sunshine and watch the leaves change. It's magical.

43 WENATCHEE RIVER: ICICLE ROAD BRIDGE

TYPE: Lowland-forest river, small beach
LOCATION: Roadside just south of Leavenworth via US 2
WATER: Cold, clear, clean, blue-green
SEASON: Summer into early fall
WHO'S HERE: Kid-friendly, dog-friendly; everyone
AMENITIES: Parking; food and lodging nearby
LOCAL'S TIP: Sleeping Lady Resort, just up Icicle Creek Road, has excellent food, coffee, and resort-style lodging and relaxation. Treat yourself!
GPS COORDINATES: 47.5771 N, −120.6744 W

Located right under the Icicle Road bridge, this spot is great for quick access and quick dips to refresh.

On US Highway 2 in Leavenworth, drive south on Icicle Road/Forest Road 7600 less than a mile. Right before the bridge over the Wenatchee, turn left into a parking lot (maybe twelve cars max).

This spot on the Wenatchee is the farthest one upriver that is still in the town of Leavenworth, yet it's off the main highway (US Highway 2), on Icicle Road. This is the preferred spot for those who launch an inner tube on their own (rather than hiring a shuttle company) and ride the river down to the main town beach (Swim #44). Don't drop your tube in above this point, because upriver is some really dangerous whitewater.

This spot is not likely to be crowded because there is limited parking and not a ton of beach real estate. From the parking lot, you're spitting distance from the water. You don't necessarily have to tube; instead, you can hang out on the small beach and swim. Because most people don't stop here, you'll likely see not more than two or three people setting up for a longer stay. It's great for a quick icy plunge after a hike from the Icicle Road trailheads before going into Leavenworth for a beer and a schnitzel.

44 WENATCHEE RIVER: LEAVENWORTH TOWN BEACH

TYPE: Lowland river, beach
LOCATION: Roadside in city park in Leavenworth via US 2
WATER: Cold to cool, clear, clean, blue-green
SEASON: Summer into early fall
WHO'S HERE: Kid-friendly; everyone, tubers
AMENITIES: Parking (with portable toilet in season); food and lodging nearby
LOCAL'S TIP: Many upstream tubers exit the river at Leavenworth's main town beach. There's at least one company (maybe a couple) that rents inner tubes and provides shuttling so you can tube downriver through town to this point.
GPS COORDINATES: 47.5941 N, –120.6565 W

GETTING THERE

From US Highway 2 in Leavenworth, find Waterfront Park off of Main Street and park in the main lot.

This spot on the Wenatchee River is basically within the town of Leavenworth and truly, no matter where you are within the heart of Leavenworth, you're only a couple blocks away from the water. The river corridor is protected by town's Waterfront Park.

When you need a break from the brats and beers, walk down here from downtown Leavenworth.

From the park's big lot right off of Main Street, walk a couple blocks to the river. Though there are a few access points to choose from, this one has a beach that is bigger and broader, and therefore it accommodates the most people. This is where it's at if you're looking for a scene. However, if you come after Labor Day, when hints of fall are in the air, it'll likely be less crowded, occupied by just a few loungers and waders. Whether you're pro- or anti-crowd, this is the nicest beach on the Wenatchee River.

The park's main parking lot can also be used to access Waterfront Park's whole trail system, which interfaces with the town in different areas. Just head south toward the river on Division Street, Commercial Street (west of Eighth), or Enchantment Park Way and you'll quickly find yourself in Waterfront Park's trail system. If you are already in town celebrating one of the Bavarian customs, such as brats, beers, or lederhosen, the park can be your launching point to explore town.

ICICLE CREEK: BRIDGE CREEK CAMPGROUND

TYPE: Mountain-forest creek, eddy, current, beach
LOCATION: Short walk in Okanogan–Wenatchee National Forest southwest of Leavenworth via US 2 and Icicle Road
WATER: Very cold to cold, clear, clean, blue-green
SEASON: Late summer to early fall
WHO'S HERE: Kid-friendly, dog-friendly; recreationists, rock climbers, campers
AMENITIES: Campground, outhouse, drinking water, picnic tables
NOTE: Northwest Forest Pass required
LOCAL'S TIP: Do a day hike in the Enchantments, then stop here after.
GPS COORDINATES: 47.5628 N, –120.7825 W

A lovely little spot to camp, picnic, or just take a quick dip on "the Icicle"

GETTING THERE

From US Highway 2 in Leavenworth, turn south onto Icicle Road/Forest Road 76. After 8.3 miles, look for a couple small pullouts on the left just before the entrance to Bridge Creek Campground. There is no day-use parking in the campground, so park here and walk into the campground to reach the creek.

Locals call it "the Icicle." As in, "We're heading up to the Icicle; see you there." In a region that is very well known and well-regarded within the outdoor recreation community, this spot is awesome not only because of the swimming itself but also because it's close to some epic hikes. There are lots of other activities too, such as whitewater kayaking and rock climbing in the valley.

Now for the disclaimer: Icicle Creek runs at high flow quite late into the season because of the glaciers out of the Enchantment Peaks and Stuart Range. The creek has a pretty big drainage, so it takes a while for it to get down to safe swimming levels. Wait until later in the year. That said, if the water is low, then it's just fine. But beware: a dangerous whitewater rapid, that even the expert kayakers portage, is located downstream of this campground, so don't take a chance. As always, don't go into water you're not sure you can get out of.

From where you parked, either hike the road or walk the unmarked but well-beaten trail for about 0.2 mile into Bridge Creek Campground and find a little trail just downstream of campsite #1 (right before a gate). As you enter the campground, this is the last campsite—and the best one in terms of catching the most sun and being right on the water. If you camp here, though, this could be a downside—people might walk through your site to get to the creek, instead of using the trail to walk from the campground road 50 feet to the water. If you are a day-tripper, please be respectful of those occupying the campsite.

The short trail down to the water takes you to a bend in the creek. As often happens in river bends, the current pushes to the outside, creating a little eddy on the inside part of the turn. Its slow current allows sand to deposit and build up on the shore, making a little beach. A big rock wall on the other side gives this area a walled-in, private feel. Pack a bucket and shovel if you and/or your kids are into erecting sand castles, but leave big water toys at home—when the water is safe, it's also too shallow for those to be useful.

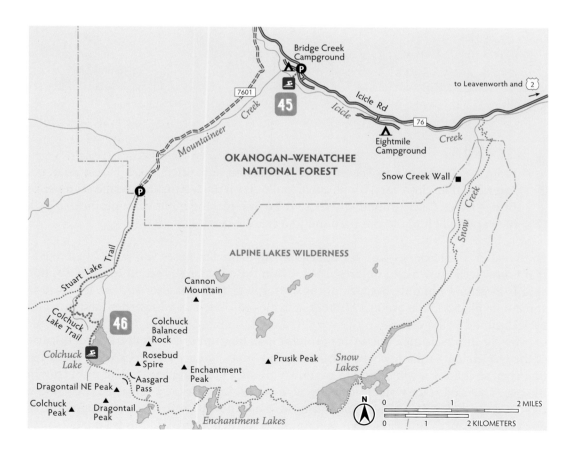

Don't bring a sun tent, either, because there's enough room for only two or three small groups, a dozen people at most, and you don't want to be that jerk hogging all the space. There aren't any cliffs to jump off (and the water shouldn't be high enough for that to be feasible anyway), but there are some big rocks to push off.

Besides Bridge Creek Campground, which is quite small and therefore fills up quickly, there are other campgrounds in Icicle Canyon. Eightmile, the first one from Leavenworth, is popular and by reservation only, so plan ahead. All the other campgrounds up Icicle Canyon are first-come, first served, and there are surely dozens more swimming holes up the Icicle begging to be discovered.

 ## 46 COLCHUCK LAKE

TYPE: Subalpine lake
LOCATION: Hike-in in Alpine Lakes Wilderness southwest of Leavenworth via US 2 and Icicle Road
WATER: Very cold, very clear, very clean, aquamarine
SEASON: Summer into early fall
WHO'S HERE: Hikers, backpackers, trail runners, a few ambitious teenagers
AMENITIES: Backcountry camping
NOTES: Hiking available nearly year-round—Northwest Forest Pass required; backcountry camping limited to June 15–October 15, with wilderness permit required in advance
LOCAL'S TIP: To camp in the Enchantments, you have to enroll in an annual lottery held in the early spring on the US Forest Service website to get a permit. If you win, don't forget toilet paper and a little pack shovel so you can Leave No Trace. See Resources at the back of this book.
GPS COORDINATES: 47.5274 N, –120.8209 W (trailhead); 47.4950 N, –120.8351 W (swimming hole)

> ### GETTING THERE
>
> From US Highway 2 on the western side of Leavenworth, turn south onto Icicle Road/Forest Road 76. After 8.4 miles, turn left onto unpaved FR 7600 and in 0.1 mile, bear right onto FR 7601. Drive 3.7 miles, watching for potholes on this slow and rocky drive. Park at Stuart Lake trailhead No. 1599. Follow Stuart Lake Trail (#1599) and Colchuck Lake Trail (1599.1) approximately 4 miles (elevation gain: 2300 feet; high point: 5600 feet).

Colchuck Lake is on the Stuart Lake Trail, part of the illustrious Enchantment Lakes of the Alpine Lakes Wilderness in Washington's Central Cascades. Depending on where you enter the Enchantments, Colchuck Lake can be either your final stop at the subalpine waters or

The enchanting waters of Colchuck Lake—one of the many lakes within the Enchantments Mountain Range (photo by Christopher Matthias)

the first taste of the many beauties to come. It's completely possible to enjoy fresh, glacier-fed Colchuck Lake à la carte if you're keeping your trip to a day hike. Backpackers can have it as an appetizer to the rest of the Enchantments and Snow Lakes.

From the trailhead parking lot, you immediately enter the wilderness area on the Stuart Lake Trail on a path that starts out on cedar duff along Mountaineer Creek, under heavy foliage and across the occasional log bridge over brisk-flowing creeks. At 1.8 miles the switchbacks begin, leading steeply up through forest and granite another 2 miles or so to the lake. Those lugging a backpack with gear to last several days will find the 2300-foot gain substantially harder than those making a day trip to Colchuck Lake; it took our excited and heavily geared group three hours to reach the first breathtaking view of the lake. Our plan was to camp at Colchuck, since the next stage of the hike is up the formidable Aasgard Pass.

Following the trail around the western edge of the lake, you'll discover a beautiful slab of granite that slopes into the water. There you can take in the warmth of the sun on your face while wading into the icy-cold water. The depth and clarity of the water will tempt brave swimmers—those who aren't afraid of the low temperatures. Cast a line—even if the fish don't bite, there is plenty to look at: the bleached pines; the snowfields of Aasgard Pass, Dragontail Peak, and Cannon Mountain.

Plan ahead and carry up an inflatable raft to enjoy the view from the middle of the lake. Even when you're sharing the area with others, there's plenty of room to spread out, and any human-made noise leaves no mark on the wide-open sky and the busy quiet of the surrounding natural world. The relative solitude in such an awe-inspiring spot is definitely worth jumping through hoops to obtain permits and making the challenging hike up.

After your swim, if you're day hiking, simply descend the Stuart Lake Trail back to the trailhead. If you're backpacking, a respite at Colchuck might just give you what you need to face Aasgard. In the morning, after scrambling over the enormous boulder field at the southern point of Colchuck Lake, then heading up the long, straight ascent over the scree of Aasgard, turn back to look onto the lake. With great height comes great visibility, and that's one beautiful lake.

47 WENATCHEE RIVER: AT DRYDEN

TYPE: Lowland river, current, beach
LOCATION: Roadside on state-managed land southeast of Leavenworth via US 2/US 97
WATER: Cold, clearish, cleanish, blue-green
SEASON: Summer into fall
WHO'S HERE: Kid-friendly, dog-friendly; migrant farmworkers, Cashmere locals
AMENITIES: Parking; food nearby
NOTE: Discover Pass required
LOCAL'S TIP: You're in Washington apple country, so check out Blake's Orchard and Cider Mill.
GPS COORDINATES: 47.5407 N, −120.5474 W

GETTING THERE

FROM LEAVENWORTH: Drive southeast on US Highway 2 toward Cashmere and Wenatchee, passing the junction with US 97 on the right. After 6.2 miles, turn left onto Dryden Avenue. **FROM BLEWETT PASS:** At the junction of US 97 and US 2, turn right (east) and after 2.7 miles, turn left onto Dryden Avenue. **FROM EITHER DIRECTION:** Drive about 0.2 mile on Dryden Avenue, then turn right onto Main Street. In less than 0.1 mile, turn left onto Depot Road and cross the railroad tracks. After 0.4 mile Depot Road becomes Raptor Lane. After about 0.3 mile, park at a wide-open but mostly undeveloped parking lot.

The Dryden swimming hole can be accessed from western Washington via Interstate 90 through Snoqualmie Pass and US Highway 97 over Blewett Pass, or via US 2 over Stevens Pass through Leavenworth. To get to this spot, you drive through the industrial stretch of US 2 between Leavenworth and Cashmere, down streets lined with warehouses in which apples are processed and boxed to be shipped around the world. The surrounding area is planted in all kinds of apple orchards. So, yes, you feel like you're in the middle of the Apple Capital of the World.

From the parking area, follow well-beaten paths up onto the levee, which is surrounded by trees and bushes, and hop over the levee to get to a long, skinny, sandy beach, 50–100 feet from the parking area. (Or keep walking up- or downriver to look for other spots.)

If the river's up, don't go swimming; it's not safe. But the water will always have a current, and when it's low you can do the whole treadmill-like cycle of swimming upstream, then allowing the current to carry you back down. This is a popular spot for the locals, whether they are commuting up or down the valley to work in the orchards or one of the many tourism-based industries.

The nice sandy beach at Dryden on the Wenatchee River

Dryden is also where many people start or stop a float trip on the Wenatchee using any number of vessels—rafts, kayaks, stand-up paddleboards—so you'll probably see boaters here as well as swimmers.

48 WENATCHEE RIVER: RODEO HOLE

TYPE: Lowland river, pools
LOCATION: Roadside southeast of Leavenworth via US 2/US 97
WATER: Cold, clearish, cleanish, blue-green
SEASON: Late summer into early fall
WHO'S HERE: Kid-friendly, dog-friendly; locals, mix of everyone
AMENITIES: Parking, restrooms
LOCAL'S TIP: Pick up some Aplets and Cotlets in Cashmere, just downstream.
GPS COORDINATES: 47.5315 N, –120.5326 W

GETTING THERE

From US Highway 2 in Leavenworth, drive east for 6.6 miles. Turn right onto Stine Hill Road, travel 1.7 miles, and turn left on Stines (plural) Hill Road. Drive 0.1 mile to a parking lot (room for more than twenty cars) on the left.

Rodeo Hole is the farthest swimming hole on the Wenatchee downstream from Leavenworth that we feature; it's almost to the town of Cashmere. Leavenworth is on the expensive side (lederhosen don't grow on trees, you know!), whereas this area is more popular with the agricultural working community. Rodeo Hole does have a restroom, but on the whole it's a little more run-down than other swimming spots in this chapter. There are patches of poison oak, too, so be careful about wandering around in the bushes. Don't let that dissuade you, though; this is a nice spot if you want to avoid the crowds around the Leavenworth tourism complex or you're looking for a place where the kiddos and dogs can run a little wilder, as there is more space here than at the other spots on the Wenatchee.

When the water's up, generally from late spring until early summer, Rodeo Hole has a swift current that forms a big hydraulic, with a giant wave and smaller waves that kayakers love. Consider checking out this spot in the spring if you want to watch the kayakers do their thing, but what this means for swimmers is, wait until the late summer, when the water is low.

From the parking lot, walk a stone's throw to the river. As the water levels drop, granite shelves start to appear. Upstream of these shelves, smaller wading pools form, perfect for younger kids. Downstream, the rock slopes into the water and extends up into the shoreline, creating something of a bench to sit on. This slope also provides easy access into a bigger, deeper pool.

Locals love the gravelly beach for lunchtime picnicking. This is a great spot if you want to set up for the day with your barbecue and cooler or other items that are hard to pack a distance. Tubers or rafters could potentially launch from here and float down to Cashmere—but please make sure the water is low enough before attempting this.

The rock slab that makes big whitewater during high-water snowmelt offers a nice place to lounge during low water.

Cascadia is defined by rugged peaks, dense forests, and lovely rivers, like the Sauk. (Swim #51)

MOUNTAIN LOOP HIGHWAY

THE MOUNTAIN LOOP HIGHWAY extends east into the Mount Baker–Snoqualmie National Forest from the Puget Sound area. From Snohomish, on US Highway 2 east of Everett, State Route 92 heads northeast to Granite Falls, where the south side of the Mountain Loop Highway begins, heading east along the South Fork Stillaguamish River. At Barlow Pass, the highway turns north along the South Fork Sauk River to the townsite of Bedal, which marks its easternmost point. Here the North Fork Sauk River meets the South Fork to form the mainstem Sauk River.

From Bedal, the Mountain Loop Highway runs northwest to Darrington in the north, then SR 530 heads west along the North Fork Stillaguamish River, to close the loop at Arlington on SR 9 northeast of Marysville. The Mountain Loop Highway provides access to several wilderness areas: Boulder River, Henry M. Jackson, and Glacier Peak wildernesses. The highway connects to the North Cascades, too—at Darrington, SR 530 heads north to SR 20 at Rockport.

49 LAKE TWENTYTWO

TYPE: Mountain-forest lake
LOCATION: Hike-in in Lake Twentytwo Research Natural Area east of Granite Falls via SR 9, SR 92, and Mountain Loop Highway
WATER: Cold, clearish, clean, blue-green
SEASON: June through October
WHO'S HERE: Kid-friendly, leashed-dog–friendly; aspiring hikers, families, dogs
AMENITIES: Parking, outhouse; picnic area, camping nearby
NOTE: Northwest Forest Pass required
LOCAL'S TIP: Stop at Barbeque Bucket in Granite Falls for some killer barbecue (shredded pork).
GPS COORDINATES: 48.0772 N, −121.7458 W (parking); 48.0668 N, −121.7624 W (swimming hole)

A day that doesn't inspire swimming, but does keep the crowds down

GETTING THERE

From I-5 in Everett, take US Highway 2 east 2.1 miles to Snohomish, then State Route 204 northeast for 2.1 miles. Turn onto SR 9 north for 1.8 miles to SR 92 east past Lake Stevens; follow this 8.3 miles northeast to Granite Falls. Continue on SR 92 through a few roundabouts. It becomes East Stanley Street. Go east for 0.3 mile, then turn left (north) onto North Alder Avenue, which becomes the Mountain Loop Highway. Drive east for 10.6 miles and enter the Mount Baker–Snoqualmie National Forest. Go through Verlot, and at 2.1 miles past the national forest boundary, pass over Twentytwo Creek. After 0.4 mile, turn right at the entry for the Lake Twentytwo trailhead No. 702 and a gravel parking lot (room for fifty or so cars). Follow the Lake Twentytwo Trail 2.75 miles (elevation gain: 1400 feet; high point: 2400 feet).

The name Lake Twentytwo, which comes from a grid system used in land surveys in the 1800s, may be drab, but the lake itself is anything but. This is a protected site—in 1947, it was established as a Research Natural Area, and so it has been untouched by loggers since then. The hike to Lake Twentytwo is challenging enough to be considered a real hike but still accessible to a new hiker building stamina or an experienced hiker looking for something mellower than usual. And there are kids. Also dogs on leashes, parents with babies strapped to their chests or backs, college students out for a breath of fresh air, perhaps hoping for a hike that will act as a hangover cure. This trail is popular, and sometimes the sound of wind in trees and birds chirping is overtaken by pop music coming from someone's phone as they walk by. This is a hike for folks who are fit enough and want to be fitter, who aren't going for total solitude, and who appreciate a beautiful scenic drive not far from the urban lowlands.

From the parking lot, the trail starts slow, underneath a canopy of looming cedars and hemlocks. You quickly start ascending; some sections of the trail have wooden stair-ramp

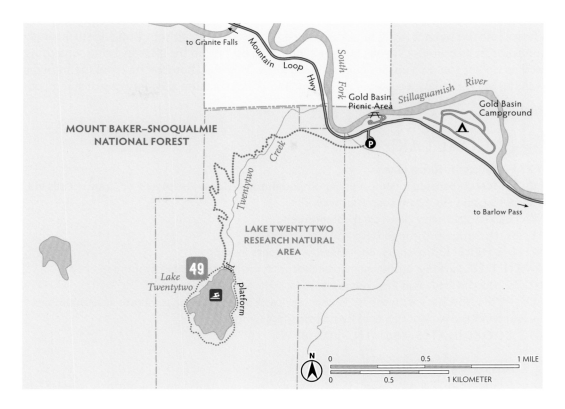

hybrids, while others are more on the rocky side. This is especially true as you get closer to the top—having healthy ankles and knees is a good idea, since you'll be picking your way and climbing over rocks big and small. For adults, focus is required, but for kids it might have an exciting playground-like feel.

Along the way, you'll pass several waterfalls and great lookout spots to the side of the trail that make a good photo op. Do be careful—it can be slippery. Depending on the season, you might have to navigate stepping-stones through trickling waterfalls that bisect the trail or duck underneath a downed tree. But this trail is pretty well maintained, even in the winter months. No matter the season, make sure your feet are prepared for water.

At 2.75 miles and 1400 feet of elevation gain, you get to the top, where a wooden platform meets the trail. Built to protect the lakeshore, it extends all the way around Lake Twentytwo's circumference. There is the occasional avalanche here, so it's best to stick to the platform and not attempt to climb the cliff sides. To the left is a wooden bridge over Twentytwo Creek. Directly across is Mount Pilchuck, covered in snow well into spring and even early summer.

The lake is small enough to walk all the way around, and it's beautiful on all sides, bordered by the face of the mountain as well as old-growth forest. From the platform, there are many entries into the water waiting to be discovered. The water, though refreshing, is surprisingly moderate in its coldness. If you can bear a little extra burden on the hike up, bring something to float on—if you do, you can push yourself away from the shoreline trail and the humans walking on it. The lake's center is where you'll find the sunshine and some peace and quiet.

50 COAL LAKE

TYPE: Mountain-forest lake
LOCATION: Roadside in Mount Baker–Snoqualmie National Forest east of Granite Falls via SR 9, SR 92, and Mountain Loop Highway
WATER: Icy cold, very clear, clean, blue-green
SEASON: Summer through fall
WHO'S HERE: Kid-friendly, dog-friendly; campers, hikers
AMENITIES: Parking, outhouse, two backcountry campsites; more camping nearby
NOTE: Northwest Forest Pass required
LOCAL'S TIP: Check with the US Forest Service to make sure the roads are accessible (see Resources at the back of this book). And bring bug spray.
GPS COORDINATES: 48.1141 N, –121.5182 W

GETTING THERE

From I-5 in Everett, take US Highway 2 east 2.1 miles to Snohomish, then State Route 204 northeast for 2.1 miles. Turn onto SR 9 north for 1.8 miles to SR 92 east past Lake Stevens; follow this 8.3 miles northeast to Granite Falls. Continue on SR 92 through a few roundabouts. It becomes East Stanley Street. Go east for 0.3 mile, then turn left (north) onto North Alder Avenue, which becomes the Mountain Loop Highway. Follow this east to milepost 26, then turn left at Perry Creek Campground and Big Four onto dirt Forest Road 4060/Coal Creek Road. Follow FR 4060 for 4.4 miles to a parking area and outhouse on the left; park here.

Coal Lake is a high mountain lake, with gloriously clear green, ice-cold water. You'll easily see the eastern brook trout and coastal cutthroat trout darting about below—the water depth is around 40 feet at its deepest. If you like fresh-caught fish roasted over a campfire, bring your fishing pole. Rumor has it that the best fishing is farther from the swimming access points, toward the steep, rocky incline to the east.

Across the road from the parking area, take the Coal Lake Trail, marked by a trailhead sign. The trail is very short, about 50 feet, though you have to climb down over some tree roots and rocks. To get to the swimming access, pass two "backcountry" campsites that sit on the west shore of the lake. The first one has a view of the water and room for two tents. The other one is a bit bigger, with room for three or four tents, and it's closer to the lakeshore. Be prepared for competition for these first-come, first-served sites.

The north shoreline at the end of the trail is dotted with big sun-warmed boulders. When we were last here, a couple had brought an inflatable raft and some floaties, though they couldn't stay too long in the water because of its low temperature. Coal Lake is very cold, very beautiful, and perfect for a short swim that will make your teeth chatter. Throw your towel across one of the boulders so that when you get out of the icy water it's heated up and ready for you. Bring a book and a picnic and spend the day lounging.

If you're in a more active mood, walk 0.1 mile up the road to the Pass Lake Trail and hike 0.4 mile to, what else, Pass Lake, or drive about 0.3 mile to the end of the road and the Independence and North Lake trailhead for a 6-mile round-trip hike. The trail to Independence Lake is 0.8 mile, with exercises in climbing over and around roots and rocks. Keep going another 2.2 miles to get to North Lake, another crystal-blue subalpine lake. At any of these lakes, you might be inspired to shrug off your pack, kick off your shoes, and get into the water to cool off. For a different way to chill, you could drive back down the road to the Mountain Loop Highway and park at the Big Four Ice Caves trailhead, then go on the easy 2.2-mile round-trip hike up to Big Four Mountain and back.

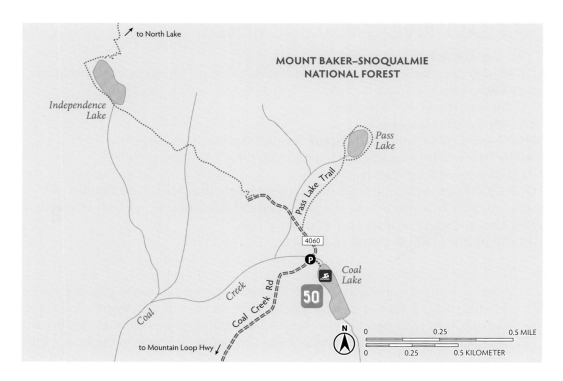

Yes, please. More mountain lakes like Coal Lake.

51 SAUK RIVER SWIMMING HOLE

TYPE: Lowland-forest river, current
LOCATION: Short walk in Mount Baker–Snoqualmie National Forest south of Darrington via SR 530 and Mountain Loop Highway
WATER: Cold, clear, clean, blue-green
SEASON: Summer into early fall
WHO'S HERE: Kid-friendly, dog-friendly; locals, fisherfolk, picnickers
AMENITIES: Parking; camping and restrooms nearby
NOTE: Northwest Forest Pass required
LOCAL'S TIP: Drive the entire Mountain Loop Highway, either via 530 and Darrington south to Granite Falls or vice versa, and give yourself plenty of time to stop and explore many of the hikes and scenic overlooks along the way.
GPS COORDINATES: 48.1708 N, −121.4738 W

GETTING THERE

From I-5 north of Marysville, take exit 208 and drive on State Route 530 east 4 miles to Arlington. Continue east on SR 530 for 28 more miles to Darrington. At a three-way stop, turn right (south) onto Forest Road 20/Mountain Loop Highway. Drive 9 miles, crossing the Sauk River near White Chuck Campground, to the Beaver Lake trailhead on the right; park here.

Dive into all that the Mountain Loop Highway offers, such as this little gem on the Sauk River.

As you relax in the sunshine listening to the Sauk River roll on by, it's easy to forget that you are only a three-minute walk from your car or that the Mountain Loop Highway is just around the corner. This favorite fishing spot among locals (be respectful, because they were there first) *feels* like it is much more remote than it actually is. The large-pebbled beach, which catches a good amount of midday sun, provides a small but efficient lounge area. Don't forget to bring a beach-read and a picnic.

After parking, start down the Beaver Lake Trail for roughly 50 feet to the first turn. There you'll see a faint trail break off to the right: follow this trail less than 0.2 mile directly to where the pebbly beach turns into river. Here, you won't find the deepest of swim spots in this book, nor does it offer the most panoramic of views, but the tall big-leaf maples, cedars, and firs dapple the water with light photogenically later in the day. Just look up: you'll see a slice of Pugh Mountain to the southeast in the distance.

Sheltered by trees on all sides, the river's glass-bottle green is worth seeing—in fact, if green is your thing, then this is definitely the spot for you. Practically each shade on the spectrum is represented, depending on the time of year, the light, and the vegetation, from moss to apple to pistachio to lime. Here you'll find a steady current, enough to swim against or float down from upstream. If you bring flotation toys, be careful and pay attention, so you don't get swept downstream in a hurry where the current picks up, with rocks right around the bend.

Though this is not a great place for rock jumping, there are one or two spots where, on a prime day, the water is deep enough to take the plunge. However, on the whole, it's just not that deep, so keep your swimming mostly at the surface. The refreshing chill will cool you off after a sweaty scenic drive over the Mountain Loop Highway or after a mellow hike along one of the many trails around Darrington. You could also consider hiking 1.3 miles up to marshy Beaver Lake to make more of your stop at this little roadside attraction.

Why cliff jump when you can tree jump!
(Swim #53)

SAN JUAN ISLANDS

THE SAN JUAN ISLANDS ARE located in the Strait of Juan de Fuca west of Samish Bay, which is south of the city of Bellingham. The arbitrary border that separates the United States from Canada is also in these waters. Only San Juan Island, Orcas Island, Lopez Island, and Shaw Island are accessible by Washington State Ferries, though other islands can be reached via smaller commuter ferries. Anacortes, on Fidalgo Island north of Whidbey Island, is the launch point for the San Juan ferries, and south of town you'll find a swim spot at Whistle Lake.

Orcas Island is truly a treasure of the Northwest. Compared to the other San Juan islands, which have uniform topography and are pretty flat, Orcas offers more mountainous terrain. On the west side of the island is Turtleback Mountain—not exactly a mountain, more like a substantial hill, at 930 feet. On the other side is Mount Constitution, which is more than 2400 feet high, higher even than Snoqualmie Pass. Drive—or hike or bike—through Moran State Park, underneath big old-growth firs and cedars, to the peak of Mount Constitution to see a breathtaking view, one of best in Washington. At the top, on a clear day you can see north to Canada and Vancouver Island, all of the San Juans, and south to Mount Rainier and the Olympic Peninsula.

Here, in Moran State Park, you'll find some pretty epic lake swimming—and more than 33 miles of smooth, well-maintained trails; runners, hikers, and mountain bikers come from far and wide to visit. While some of the trails are open to mountain biking all year, fall is the best time for biking; during the spring and summer some of the trails are closed to bikers to make way for more hikers. Like all the San Juans, Orcas is a popular road-biking destination too.

 ## THE LAGOON (ORCAS ISLAND)

TYPE: Lowland lake
LOCATION: Short walk or hike-in in Moran State Park on Orcas Island via SR 20 and Washington State Ferries

WATER: Cold to warm, clearish, cleanish, blue-green
SEASON: Year-round
WHO'S HERE: Kid-friendly, dog-friendly; locals, camp kids
AMENITIES: Parking; camping, food, and lodging nearby
NOTE: Discover Pass required
LOCAL'S TIP: Orcas Food Co-op in Eastsound is small but great, and they carry fresh oysters and clams daily.
GPS COORDINATES: 48.6513 N, –122.8653 W

GETTING THERE

From I-5 at Burlington, take exit 230 onto State Route 20 westbound 19.2 miles through Anacortes, following signs to the Washington State Ferries dock west of town. Take the ferry to Orcas Island, and after departing the ferry at the Orcas Island ferry terminal, turn left onto Orcas Road (Horseshoe Highway). After 8.1 miles, turn right onto Main Street in Eastsound. At 0.4 mile, the road name changes to Crescent Beach Drive. After 0.9 mile, turn right onto Olga Road. After 3.1 miles, turn onto Rosario Road. After 0.5 mile, turn left onto Palisades Drive and in about 0.1 mile park beside some old tennis courts. The hike-in to the bridge is about 0.4 mile one way (elevation gain: minimal; high point: about 200 feet).
BY BIKE: Bike onto the Anacortes ferry (you save a lot of money and won't have to wait in line either) and at the Orcas ferry terminal, wait until the cars have dispersed before following the flow of traffic along Horseshoe Highway on the 13-mile car route described above.

The Lagoon is technically part of Cascade Lake, like an alcove is technically part of a room. If you look at this book's map, you'll see that the Lagoon sticks out like a claw from the bigger body of water's west side. The Lagoon catches the evening sun, nice on those Northwest summer days when night doesn't fall until after 8:00 p.m. If you are running late, or the air temperature is a touch cooler, choose the Lagoon for a late-in-the-day dip. This is the easy go-to drop-by spot for locals, and it does feel more casual (and a bit easier for dogs) than the other Orcas Island swims.

From the Lagoon parking, follow the obvious trail system, staying right at the forks to the Lagoon. In 0.2 mile you come to the first rock outcropping, which sticks out from the forest into the water's edge. This is that quick drop-by dip spot. About 100–200 feet farther along are one or two more rock outcroppings.

The Lagoon is similar to Cascade Lake (Swim #53), since they are both the same body of water, but each has its own unique characteristics. The Lagoon is shallower and pinched-off enough from Cascade Lake to feel like its own small universe, and because of this it warms up more quickly.

Enjoying the end of the day at the Lagoon on Orcas Island—a spot that catches great late-day sun

If you walk for about another 0.25 mile you get to a beautiful bridge, just under 0.5 mile from where you parked. This well-known bridge is made of big timber logs, strong and sturdy and perfect for jumping off. It's the right height—roughly 10 feet—to make some people nervous, some excited, some both, and the water underneath is just deep enough. Daredevils can jump off the railing, but most people go off the edge. Be mindful—it really is *just* deep enough. From here you can retrace your steps or continue on the trail around the lagoon about 0.4 mile to return to the parking area.

If you're cycling to the Lagoon and you'd like a little more space and less exhaust fumes, from Horseshoe Highway take Deer Harbor Road West through West Sound to Crow Valley Road. This takes you north to rejoin Horseshoe Highway a mile or so south of Eastsound, or you can take the more scenic Enchanted Valley Road west for a short detour through West Beach, where you can stop if you need a break (or a consolation prize). Going the Crow Valley Road direct to Horseshoe Highway adds about 2 miles; taking Crow Valley and the Enchanted Valley Road adds about 3 miles.

53 CASCADE LAKE (ORCAS ISLAND)

TYPE: Lowland lake
LOCATION: Roadside or hike-in in Moran State Park on Orcas Island via SR 20 and Washington State Ferries
WATER: Cold to cool, clearish, cleanish, blue-green
SEASON: Year-round
WHO'S HERE: Kid-friendly, dog-friendly; everyone
AMENITIES: Parking, restrooms, picnic areas, ice-cream stand, paddleboat rentals; camping nearby
NOTE: Discover Pass required
LOCAL'S TIP: Stop in at Spy Hop Subs on your way through Eastsound to grab a couple subs for a picnic.
GPS COORDINATES: 48.6555 N, –122.8539 W

GETTING THERE

From I-5 at Burlington, take exit 230 onto State Route 20 westbound 19.2 miles through Anacortes, following signs to the Washington State Ferries dock west of town. Take the ferry to Orcas Island, and after departing the ferry at the Orcas Island ferry terminal, turn left onto Orcas Road (Horseshoe Highway). After 8.1 miles, turn right onto Main Street in Eastsound. After 0.4 mile, the road name changes to Crescent Beach Drive. After 0.9 mile, turn right onto Olga Road and soon enter Moran State Park. After 3.7 miles, turn right into the big day-use parking lot. The hike-in is 0.5 mile (or more) one way, or a 2.7-mile loop (elevation gain: minimal; high point about 300 feet). **BY BIKE:** See Getting There for the Lagoon (Swim #52), but instead of turning on Rosario Road, continue on Olga Road to the Cascade Lake day-use area, about 13 miles from the ferry dock.

Cascade Lake is the biggest body of freshwater on Orcas Island, located near the west entrance to Moran State Park. On Olga Road, you drive by a big grassy beach. Don't worry, you'll see it—you really can't miss it. Near the big parking lot, there's a dock with paddleboats to rent, as well as picnic areas and even an ice-cream shack. Bring your fishing gear and drop a line here—fishing season starts at the end of April, and the lake is stocked every year with rainbow, kokanee, and cutthroat trout.

This public beach is the most developed section of the park, but there are plenty of big evergreen trees around, and you'll still feel very much surrounded by nature. If your idea of swimming involves lots of accessories (coolers, SUPs, beach chairs, blankets, etc.) that

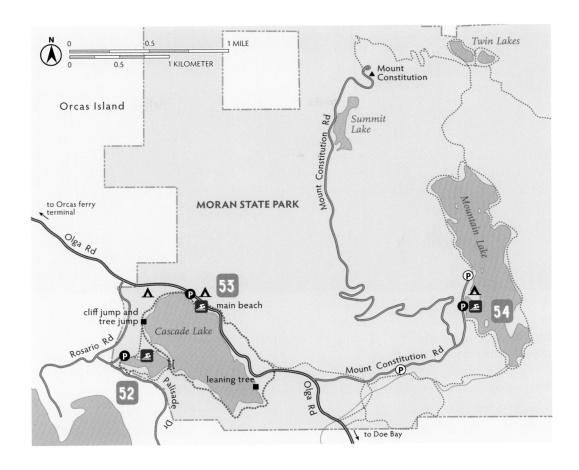

you don't want to carry too far, this is the spot for you. There's enough space for everyone to do their thing.

Cascade Lake also offers a 2.7-mile loop trail around its circumference, which will take you far away from the public-beach hubbub and to dozens of great spots to get into the water. If you walk the trail counterclockwise from the public beach, after 0.5 mile you come to a beautiful full-scale bonsai-like tree that's growing out of a rock. Instead of cliff jumping, there's tree jumping: show off some of your gymnastic skills by crawling up onto it, then jumping off into the deep blue water. You can also jump off shoreline cliffs, but they're not a straight vertical, so do make sure you have enough clearance.

Keep walking counterclockwise around Cascade Lake for another 0.4 mile and you'll come to the Lagoon (Swim #52) and its popular bridge. Or you can keep walking for

SUP?! on Cascade Lake.

another mile to another tree leaning almost horizontally out over the water, perfect for some balance-beam training.

To complete the loop around the lake, the trail heads inland through the trees, but everywhere you look, you'll see gorgeous Northwest greens and blues.

54 MOUNTAIN LAKE (ORCAS ISLAND)

TYPE: Lowland-forest lake, islands
LOCATION: Roadside in Moran State Park on Orcas Island via SR 20 and Washington State Ferries
WATER: Cold to cool, clear, cleanish, blue-green
SEASON: Spring into fall
WHO'S HERE: Kid-friendly, dog-friendly; locals, summer-camp kids, tourists
AMENITIES: Parking, restrooms, dock, campground; hiking, mountain biking, and horseback riding trails
NOTE: Discover Pass required
LOCAL'S TIP: Take a hot tub and sauna at the Doe Bay Resort, then grab a delicious, fresh organic meal at the Doe Bay Café.
GPS COORDINATES: 48.6570 N, −122.8184 W

GETTING THERE

From I-5 at Burlington, take exit 230 onto State Route 20 westbound and continue 19.2 miles through Anacortes, following signs to the Washington State Ferries dock west of town. Take the ferry to Orcas Island, and after departing the ferry at the Orcas Island ferry terminal, follow Orcas Road (Horseshoe Highway) north. After 8.1 miles, turn right onto Main Street in Eastsound. After 0.4 mile, the road name changes to Crescent Beach Drive. At 0.4 mile, turn right onto Olga Road, then continue south another 3.7 miles into Moran State Park and pass by Cascade Lake (pick up the trail map). After about 1 mile take a left on the Mount Constitution Road, in 0.7 mile turn right toward Mountain Lake, and in 0.25 mile reach a parking lot at the lakeshore (room for roughly twelve cars). If it's full, park on the road shoulder or continue on the campground road, which becomes easy-to-travel dirt and after about 0.25 mile splits between two giant cedar trees at another parking area (room for eight cars), with a boat launch and campground. Or drive back downhill to Mountain Lake Landing and park at the trailhead, then hike about a mile up to the lake. **BY BIKE**: See Getting There for the Lagoon (Swim #52), but instead of turning onto Rosario Road, continue on Olga Road to the Cascade Lake day-use area. From here, it's an uphill 2 miles to the Mountain Lake swimming hole (you could also add a steep 4.3-mile ride to the top of Mount Constitution and have a fun ride back down to the lake for a swim afterward).

Our favorite spot in the Moran State Park area is Mountain Lake because of its higher elevation. It feels more end-of-the-road and untouched. The water is a little colder, too, but it's still really quite comfortable for swimming. Even though many people choose to bike here, sometimes the parking areas fill up; if necessary, park down the hill and run or hike up the trail to the lake.

The main parking area is on the lake's shadier west side. The other parking area is at the Mountain Lake Campground; you could reserve one of the six campsites here—they're relatively close to one another, right up from the boat launch.

There is a dock at the main parking lot, so you can bring your canoe, kayak, or stand-up paddleboard to launch here. You can paddle out or swim to one or both of the two mini-islands within Mountain Lake that are easy to swim out to. It's "very meta," said a friend, referring to being on an island in a lake on an island in Puget Sound.

You can also walk the pleasant, flat, 3.9-mile trail around the lake to find a sunnier spot—there's plenty of room, though of course the areas with the most sunshine tend to fill up the fastest. Explore all the various nooks and crannies along the shoreline—anywhere you land, the water will be clean, clear, and cold.

Island Time at Mountain Lake

Keep an eye out for a rope swing—we won't say exactly where for a couple of reasons: One, according to some locals, it often gets taken down and therefore it might not be there no matter how hard you look. And two, there is something to be said for not giving away all the secrets. Another idea: A local at the Mountain Lake rope swing told us that he often goes to the Lagoon and Cascade Lake on "three-lake days," but for a four-lake day, he takes the trail from the north end of Mountain Lake 0.7 mile north to Twin Lakes; they're a little marshier, with one decent beach and one mediocre cliff jump. But it's still a chance to swim in four lakes in one day. Sounds like a good adventure to us.

55 WHISTLE LAKE (FIDALGO ISLAND)

TYPE: Lowland lake, beach, cliff jump
LOCATION: Hike-in in Anacortes Community Forest Lands south of Anacortes via
I-5 and SR 20
WATER: Cold to cool, clearish, cleanish, blue-green
SEASON: Year-round
WHO'S HERE: Kid-friendly, dog-friendly; cliff jumpers, families
AMENITIES: Parking, outhouse, garbage can
LOCAL'S TIP: Keep an eye out for wildlife—owls are known to make an appearance
every now and then.
GPS COORDINATES: 48.4626 N, –122.6051 W

GETTING THERE

From I-5 at Burlington, take exit 230 onto State Route 20 westbound toward Anacortes. In 11.4 miles, stay straight on the SR 20 Spur west toward Anacortes (not south toward Deception Pass). At the traffic circle, drive around to the second exit and turn onto Commercial Avenue. Turn right on Longview Avenue, turn left onto O Avenue, and follow it 0.8 mile through some housing. Turn left onto Spradley Road (signed for Whistle Lake). After 0.4 mile, turn right onto Whistle Lake Road, then in 0.1 mile turn left onto Whistle Lake Terrace. In less than 0.1 mile reach a Y, take the right fork, and follow the dirt road about 0.25 mile to the trailhead and park (room for ten or so cars). Follow the main lake trail 1.3 to 1.5 miles (elevation gain: 200 feet; high point: 500 feet).

Whistle Lake is within the city limits of Anacortes, close enough to the town center to bike to (follow the driving directions from the traffic circle) or even walk to if you're up for a trek. This is the town from which the San Juan Islands and Sidney, British Columbia, ferries depart. Technically, Anacortes is on Fidalgo Island, which is separated from the mainland by a little strip of water called the Swinomish Channel—named for the people who inhabited this area before the arrival of settlers in the late eighteenth century. Every now and then, this channel dries up or disappears at low tide, but even so, Fidalgo Island it is.

The Whistle Lake trailhead leads to many trails in the Anacortes Community Forest Lands, free for mountain bikers and hikers to use year-round. According to some mountain-bike experts, these trails aren't for the faint of heart—you have to "earn" them. The beautiful forest has been known to offer plenty of wildlife sightings, particularly birds of prey. The lake itself is not accessible by vehicle, so you must hike in.

At the trailhead there is a map of a vast network of trails to explore, but you're here to swim, so follow the main trail (it's actually an old road) that starts behind a big gate. Once you reach the water, about 1 mile from the parking lot, the trail forks—and at first sight, Whistle Lake looks like a marshy little nook. The lake itself is a lowland one, without a lot of inflow and outflow, so it doesn't feel as crisp as higher mountain lakes do, but it does feature some epic cliff jumping. From the fork you have two options:

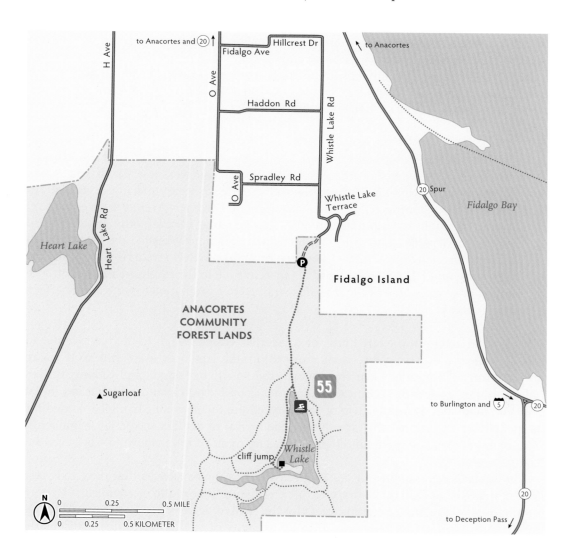

Go left, clockwise, on a continuation of the main trail along the water's edge on the east side of the lake to reach the go-to easy-access spot. As you walk, you'll be certain to find a couple spots to swim, but at about 0.3 mile from the fork, when you get to well-trampled ground and an accessible sandy, rocky point, you'll know you're at the main swimming hole, which gradually eases from shallow into deeper water. You might bump into other hikers enjoying the lake-wide vista.

Alternatively, back at the trail fork by the lakeshore, you can go right, counterclockwise, on a well-traveled, more single-track trail along the water's edge on the west side of the lake. This gives you access to many little dirt beaches and rock outcroppings from which

Whistle Lake's main beach

Solid cliff jumping at Whistle Lake

to enter the lake. When we were last there, a small rope swing hung near a bench along the trail—it's a bit on the wimpy side in terms of daredevilry.

Keep going if you want some more adventure. The popular cliff-jumping spot is on an island in the lake, so to get there, continue about 0.5 mile from the fork to where the trail is closest to the island's west end and drop your gear, swim across 100 feet or so, and climb up the viewer's-right side of the island. There's a good chance you'll see some young adults or teenagers taking the leap from the various rocky shelves. The smallest jump is at least 10 feet high. Keep in mind that jumping from any height can be dangerous.

We almost didn't make it to this swimming hole but managed to squeeze it in at the end of the day. On the trail back from Whistle Lake to the trailhead, we hiked past an owl, the closest we've ever been to one, and that alone made this swim worth it. Good lesson: it's usually worth making time for one more mission. Keep an eye out for wildlife. We've heard that bald eagles are often around too.

The Liberty Bell spires tower above
Blue Lake. (Swim #60)

NORTH CASCADES

WHEN PEOPLE SAY "North Cascades," they are usually referring to both North Cascades National Park and the more rugged northern range of the Cascades surrounding and including the park. Bisected west to east by State Route 20, which is closed in the winter, much of the North Cascades can be accessed only in the summer, and it's well worth the effort. Just by driving through this range, you can get a good sense of all the exploration opportunities in this part of the state, including Mount Baker Wilderness Area and British Columbia parkland to the north.

The mighty Skagit River flows from Ross Lake west many miles into Puget Sound south of Anacortes. Ross Lake National Recreation Area, as well as Mount Baker National Recreation Area, features big lakes and lots of outdoor activities, from camping, hiking, and boating to winter skiing. Deeper into the range, SR 20 reaches Rainy and Washington passes amid dramatic glaciated peaks. This chapter's swimming spots are not technically in the national park, but a couple are very close, just outside the boundary for a taste of this fairly remote and rugged area.

 ## 56 SKAGIT RIVER: RASAR STATE PARK

TYPE: Lowland river, current, beach
LOCATION: Short walk or hike-in in state park west of Concrete via I-5 and SR 20
WATER: Very cold to cold, milky-opaque, silty, turquoise green
SEASON: Summer into early fall
WHO'S HERE: Kid-friendly, dog-friendly; families, stand-up paddleboarders, RVers, campers, people chilling, anglers
AMENITIES: Day-use parking, restrooms, picnic tables and shelters, wheelchair access, playground, volleyball court, campground, RV dump station; food and lodging nearby
NOTE: Discover Pass required
LOCAL'S TIP: The Woolley Market in Sedro-Woolley has everything you need, from lunch to cold beverages to s'mores. Load up before for a picnic or a weekend in the mountains, or come at the end of the weekend with an empty belly.
GPS COORDINATES: 48.5149 N, –121.9043 W

GETTING THERE

From I-5 at Burlington, take exit 230 onto State Route 20 eastbound toward Concrete and drive east to milepost 80. Turn right on Lusk Road, then in 0.6 mile turn left on Cape Horn Road. After another 0.6 mile, turn right into Rasar State Park, and continue 0.6 mile to the day-use parking area. Follow park trails either 0.2 mile or about 0.5 mile (elevation gain: negligible; high point: about 300 feet).

If you're driving State Route 20 westbound after a hike in the North Cascades, you'll be paralleling the Skagit River most of the way. This beautiful river is like a siren's song or a cartoon hot apple pie cooling on the windowsill: it's hypnotizing, and you may find yourself next to the water without remembering how you got there. To quote a friend, it's "super turquoisey and awesome. Like a toothpaste commercial." This swim spot could be confused for a tropical beach if it weren't for all those telltale Douglas firs and alders—oh, and the freezing-cold water. Located in Rasar State Park, this swim spot can be a family

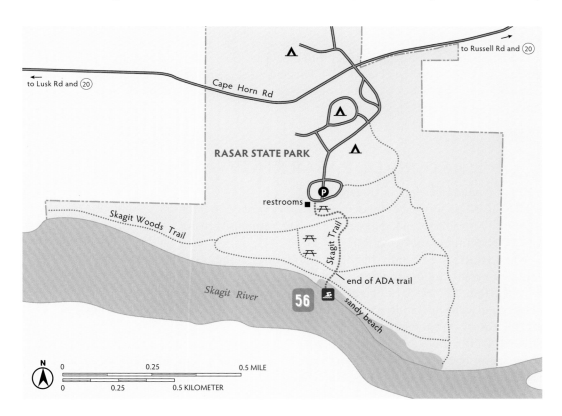

Color: Hawaii. Temperature: Washington.

picnic destination, or it can be a quick stop for cooling off, one of the last such stops if you're westbound.

From the day-use parking area, follow the wheelchair-accessible Skagit Trail south about 0.2 mile to a T near the river, then continue off-trail straight ahead about 60 feet to the water's edge. Or at the T, head left to continue about 0.25 mile on the now-dirt trail upriver until the trail turns north, then turn right, off-trail, to walk about 50 feet straight to the water's edge. The long white-sand beach between these two spots, surrounded by big evergreen trees, is an interesting contrast to that green water. The sand is clean, perfect for the kiddos and their sand-castle aspirations.

As mentioned above, the water is cold, real cold, as in an 8 on a scale of 1 to 10. Plus there's a fair bit of current. Advanced stand-up paddleboarders can head to the upstream spot and take out at the downstream spot—you'll really get those abs working. Likewise, if you bring out the inner tube, you're gonna move, so be careful: it's easy to flow with the river beyond the extent of the park and into farmland.

While you're here, check out the 169-acre state park, which includes shady forested trails, sheltered picnic areas, big grassy fields, dog-friendly and kid-friendly activities, and lots of places to roam. Of the thirty-eight campsites, twenty have electricity, and some are walk-in or hiker-biker sites. Don't forget your bird- and elk-watching binoculars and your fishing pole.

57 BACON CREEK

TYPE: Lowland-forest creek, pool
LOCATION: Roadside in Mount Baker–Snoqualmie National Forest east of Marblemount via I-5 and SR 20
WATER: Very cold, very clear, very clean, blue-green
SEASON: Summer into early fall
WHO'S HERE: Kid-friendly, dog-friendly; car campers, kids in tow
AMENITIES: DIY camping; other camping and food nearby
LOCAL'S TIP: Don't speed through the town of Marblemount—it's a notorious speeding trap.
GPS COORDINATES: 48.6021 N, –121.3953 W

GETTING THERE

From I-5 at Burlington, take exit 230 onto State Route 20 eastbound toward Concrete and drive east for 50.1 miles, then turn left (north) on unpaved Forest Road 1060/ Bacon Creek Road. After 0.7 mile, reach a small unmarked pullout (room for three or four cars) and park.

Set up camp so that you can wake to the crystal-clear water of Bacon Creek.

Less than a mile off State Route 20 up Bacon Creek Road, this swimming hole is convenient for those visiting the North Cascades, the Methow Valley, or the east side of Washington. A few years ago we discovered this spot after heading out from Lazy Bear Falls (Swim #58) and dropped in for a quick dip. The next year we returned and set up camp—it's a wonderful swim, especially first thing in the morning after a nice night sleeping under the stars. You could spend a chunk of time here if you were so inclined.

At the small parking pullout, there are no amenities—no picnic tables or restrooms or formal campsites—but you can put up a tent right by the creek once the snowmelt has subsided for the summer. For car campers—rather than those planning to backpack out into the wilderness—this spot is far enough off the beaten path that there's a good chance you won't get a lot of foot traffic going by. You might not run into a single stranger, but you'll likely see where other people have made campfires. Whenever possible, use an established fire ring instead of building your own, for both safety and aesthetic reasons. (See LNT in Resources.)

A small well-worn trail leads you down 50 feet or so to a cobblestone beach. At this point, you'll forget that you're near the road, because the creek will have all of your attention. Take a walk 100 feet or so downstream along the streambed, and there you are.

This Bacon Creek swimming hole is nothing fancy—there are no big cliffs or rope swings or any one feature that really stands out. But it is quintessential Northwest, with clean, crystal-clear green water and a pretty pool set in the corner of the creek, just big and deep enough to truly swim in. It's one of the colder spots we've been to, fed by glaciers on Bacon Peak, Mount Despair, and Mount Triumph.

Look for a secondary spot almost immediately upriver, a wider and calmer stretch that's not as deep. Here you could drop in an inner tube and float gently down, even going around the bend for a bit. Bring your underwater camera, swim goggles, and snorkel mask because the water is so clear.

 ## 58 FALLS CREEK: LAZY BEAR FALLS

TYPE: Lowland-forest creek, waterfall, pool
LOCATION: Short walk in Mount Baker–Snoqualmie National Forest east of Marblemount via I-5 and SR 20
WATER: Very cold, crystal clear, very clean, blue-green
SEASON: Summer into early fall
WHO'S HERE: Waterfall photographers, rednecks, ATVers
AMENITIES: Parking, fire ring
NOTES: High-clearance vehicle required, four-wheel drive recommended—potholes and overgrown vegetation on FR 1065
LOCAL'S TIP: A stop at the Cascadian Farm stand, near Rockport, for snacks is a must.
GPS COORDINATES: 48.6333 N, –121.4273 W

GETTING THERE

From I-5 at Burlington, take exit 230 onto State Route 20 eastbound toward Concrete and drive east 50.1 miles, then turn left (north) on unpaved Forest Road 1060/Bacon Creek Road. Follow FR 1060/Bacon Creek Road for 5 miles, then at a three-way fork turn left onto FR 1064 and drive down to, then over, a bridge crossing Bacon Creek. Continue up for about 0.6 mile. The road then switches back, and a fire pit should be visible on the left side. Take the road to the left, FR 1065, for 0.8 mile. Park at the turnaround.

Though it's no deserted island, Lazy Bear Falls feels remote enough to make you draw a face on something and call it Wilson. Though it's not terribly far off State Route 20, it's just outside North Cascades National Park and Mount Baker Wilderness. Be forewarned

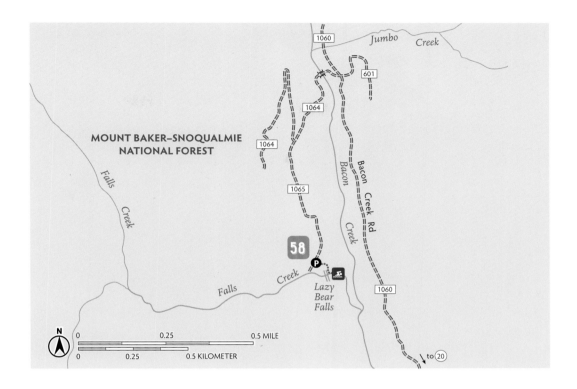

that this location does require a little determination to reach: some gigantic potholes on Bacon Creek Road and the lush overgrown vegetation as well as dips and crags on the second half of the route make the last part of the journey feel like you're driving on a loofah. A high-clearance vehicle is required, and four-wheel drive is highly recommended. You could also find an earlier pullout, park, and walk along the road if your car or driving experience is not up for the task.

From the parking area, you should be able to hear the waterfall. Since Falls Creek flows in an easterly direction, plan on getting to this spot by late morning or early afternoon to maximize time in the sun. The water temp will definitely get your attention. By midafternoon (possibly earlier in late summer or early fall), you'll have to weigh your desire to jump in against the lack of post-swim warming-up sunshine.

There is plenty of room near the parking spot to camp, though it is mostly DIY camping. The only development is a fire ring, which you can use if you're arriving in the evening in order to take advantage of the morning sun. If you are planning a weekend in the North Cascades, go here the first night, camp, and start the next day off with a swim. You'll be fully rested, relaxed, refreshed, and ready to head off to your next adventure.

It's worth the bumpy roads to get here.

From the parking area, take an unmarked, overgrown trail east about 800 feet and down about 150 feet to the falls. The trail is eroded in spots, so expect 500 feet or so of scrambling. The bumpy ride and the scramble are worth it. There are just so many fun things to do here.

The giant log that crosses the creek is ideal for balance-beam-style fun—it's wide enough to not be too scary, but narrow and high enough to feel like a challenge. Once you get to the base of the falls, the pool itself offers a plethora of enjoyable water activities: you can jump off the rocks along the shore, swim a few strokes in the just-big-enough pool, or take yourself underneath the falls for a pressure wash. If you want some quiet time, swim behind the falls, where you'll be pleasantly veiled. The water is superclear, so bring your goggles and/or underwater camera to further explore the depths of the pool.

Perhaps curiosity will get the best of you and you'll want to find out what's upstream. A faint trail to the west of the parking area gets you started, but you then need to bushwhack to fully explore. Wear footwear with good traction, or even carry some cordelette, to access the upper pools—the need for caution in and above the main falls should be obvious!

 ## SKAGIT RIVER: EAST OF MARBLEMOUNT

TYPE: Lowland-forest river, eddy, beach
LOCATION: Roadside in Mount Baker–Snoqualmie National Forest between Marblemount and Newhalem via I-5 and SR 20
WATER: Very cold to cold, clear, clean, blue-green
SEASON: Summer
WHO'S HERE: Kid-friendly, dog-friendly; locals, recreationists
AMENITIES: Parking
LOCAL'S TIP: Reserve a spot at Newhalem's Dam Good Chicken Dinner, a three-hour event during which you'll eat a traditional family-style meal, watch a slideshow about the history of hydroelectricity on the Skagit, and take an easy nighttime walking tour of Ladder Creek Gardens along the Ladder Creek Falls Trail.
GPS COORDINATES: 48.6139 N, –121.3610 W

GETTING THERE

From I-5 at Burlington, take exit 230 onto State Route 20 eastbound toward Concrete and drive east 52.4 miles. Between mile markers 114 and 113, park at a pullout (room for four or five cars max). **BY BIKE:** SR 20 is popular for road biking, so you could bike here if that's your thing.

Though State Route 20 runs parallel to the Skagit River, there aren't a lot of obvious areas to pull off for a swim. There are plenty of pullouts and access points along the river for kayaking and other whitewater play, but this is one of the few spots with a decent beach, and that's part of what makes it special. The Skagit River is big relative to other swimming rivers described in this book, but it has eye appeal—once you see the river, you'll have to get into it.

Because it's big, though, even in the late weeks of summer, there's still a fair bit of volume and current, so be careful—if you swim out into the main current, you can get pulled downstream fast. However, at this pullout there's a big eddy, which provides a buffer and plenty of room to swim in slow water—another reason this location is special.

You should never pass up an opportunity to visit this spot.

The pullout is not so obvious, and it's easier to see if you're heading eastbound and uphill. It's east of Marblemount and close to Bacon Creek (Swim #57) and Lazy Bear Falls (Swim #58), but farther up and into the mountains. If this pullout is full, you can keep driving and park at the next one, then walk back down the highway, being mindful of the traffic.

From the original pullout, hike 50 feet to the river—it's right off the highway, not so much a wilderness. That said, trees separate the highway from the river, and the nearness to the road isn't as noticeable once you're at the shore. It's a really beautiful spot, with a small sand beach that has room for a group or two. Bedrocks line both shores, welcome if you'd rather lie on rock to warm up. Per usual, you could walk up- or downriver to find your own little bit of beach.

The water is so green that it feels almost tropical—until you get in, that is. The Skagit River is exceptionally cold, so that illusion goes out the window real quick. You can slowly wade into the water, where you'll find a sandbar that acts as a good natural barrier from the main current for kids. It is likely that the sandbar forms year in and year out, but perhaps if there were a big flood that would change—like everything in the universe, rivers always change. Beyond the sandbar, the water gets deeper, and you can swim into the eddy before going out into the current.

There's also an opportunity for some advanced tubing. This section of the river has a current and some whitewater, with good entry and exit points. It's fast enough to be called river travel—great for stand-up paddleboarding or kayaking. However, if kayaking or SUPing is your main goal, pull over elsewhere and leave this spot for the beachgoers.

 ## 60 BLUE LAKE

TYPE: Alpine lake, cliff jump, small beach
LOCATION: Hike-in in Okanogan–Wenatchee National Forest west of Washington Pass via SR 20
WATER: Very cold to cold, very clear, very clean, very blue
SEASON: Midsummer through early fall
WHO'S HERE: Kid-friendly, dog-friendly; outdoorsy folks, North Cascades National Park visitors
AMENITIES: Parking, outhouse
NOTE: Northwest Forest Pass required
LOCAL'S TIP: Sign up for a class or field excursion at North Cascades Institute. Their Environmental Learning Center offers a wide range of fun learning experiences, from photography to hawk watching to mushroom hunting to wildlife tracking.
GPS COORDINATES: 48.5191 N, –120.6742 W

GETTING THERE

From I-5 near Burlington, take exit 230 onto State Route 20 eastbound toward Concrete and drive east for 71.7 miles. Turn right, into the trailhead parking area on the south side of the highway. Follow the Blue Lake Trail 2.2 miles (elevation gain: 1000 feet; high point: 6254 feet).

The blueness of this lake, its proximity to State Route 20, and its location near the summit of Washington Pass make Blue Lake especially attractive. Of course, all lakes are blue, but this one is superblue, as in stunning cobalt blue. The hike to get here is really nice too: it's not too far, at 2.2 miles, and with 1000 feet of elevation gain it's reasonable for people on both sides of the age spectrum. You'll see plenty of kids and older folks along the trail. If you're looking for a little more solitude, make the climb during odd hours, but remember that the temperature can be as much as 20 degrees Fahrenheit cooler up on Washington Pass than down in Mazama on the east side of the pass, so reserve your swimming in such cold alpine waters for the hotter days. If the day is truly hot, the water feels less teeth-chatteringly cold and more comfortably refreshing.

Did we mention that this lake is blue?

Technically this lake isn't in North Cascades National Park, but it's very close, and it's one of the more popular hikes on the North Cascades Highway. The trail makes three long switchbacks through forest, and at 1.7 miles there's a path to the left that heads to South Early Winters Spire. As you approach the lake, you'll likely see roped-off restoration areas, a good reminder of the human impact on the environment up here. Please adhere to these closures, and don't worry—there are plenty of open spots for getting in the water. When you reach a fork in the trail, stay right and go counterclockwise around the lake's west shore; pretty soon you'll come to a cliff–rock outcropping. This is a popular spot for taking photos and picnicking. You can also jump off this rock into the water—it's small, ideal for those looking for a cliff-jumping-lite experience. For most people, this is where the trip ends.

But if you want a spot away from the crowds, carry on counterclockwise around the lake to find a more beach-like zone. Here, a dirt shoreline meets rocks as you wade into the water. The water is superclear, whether you're looking down into it or you've strapped on your goggles for some fantastic underwater viewing. Don't forget your waterproof camera for underwater photography. Last time we were here, we saw one strong person who had carried his inflatable stand-up paddleboard all the way up, but for those with a little less endurance and backbone, bring a floaty instead. A field of boulders makes for many choices of rocks to sit on or near between swims.

You can continue walking counterclockwise to get some elevation above the water, where wider views give you further appreciation of the epic blueness. You can also see classic mountain-lake scenery, with the big granite Early Winters Spire dramatically poking their peaks above the tree line to the northeast. If you catch that fleeting moment before late-summer heat gives way to autumn, you'll be rewarded with the gorgeous sight of larches turning golden yellow.

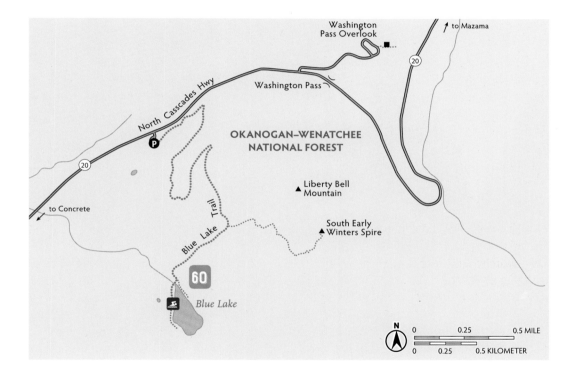

Summer daze at its finest (Swim #61)

METHOW VALLEY

THE METHOW RIVER, a tributary of the Columbia River, is more than 80 miles long and stems from the North Cascades. The Methow begins northwest of Mazama, and flows through the towns of Mazama, Winthrop, and Twisp, then down to the Columbia at Pateros.

The Methow Valley is one of the Pacific Northwest's most beloved valleys. With Washington Pass being closed in the winter, it always feels like a treat when, in the spring, State Route 20 is reopened, allowing a shortcut to all that makes this valley special: sun, warmth, views, recreation for all types, and an all-around slower, more enjoyable pace of life.

The town of Mazama is the northernmost development in the Methow Valley after you leave North Cascades National Park at Washington Pass summit. Mazama is definitely small-town, with its general store, a few Northwest-centric restaurants, a heli-ski business, a mountain guide business, a couple of outdoor outfitters, and fewer than 200 residents. This town can be either a lovely final destination—check out the lodgings, both rustic and quaint—or a detour totally worth the extra couple miles.

 ## 61 METHOW RIVER: AT MAZAMA

TYPE: Mountain-forest river, small beach
LOCATION: Roadside in Okanogan–Wenatchee National Forest near Mazama via SR 20
WATER: Cold, clear, clean, green
SEASON: Summer into early fall
WHO'S HERE: Kid-friendly, dog-friendly; recreationists, families, weekenders
AMENITIES: Parking; food and lodging nearby
LOCAL'S TIP: Stop by the Mazama Store for "Brat Night"—beer, homemade buns, bratwurst, and the works.
GPS COORDINATES: 48.6225 N, –120.4554 W

FROM WASHINGTON PASS: Head down State Route 20 for 17 miles to the Mazama turnoff and turn left. **FROM TWISP:** Head northwest on SR 20 toward Winthrop; after 22 miles, reach the Mazama turnoff and turn right. **FROM EITHER DIRECTION:** Go 0.4 mile to a T in Mazama, then turn left onto Lost River Road/ Mazama Road. After 3.2 miles reach a dirt pullout on the left and park (holds twelve or so cars).

No one's trying to keep this swimming hole a secret, yet it's maintained a mellow community vibe. In part this must be attributed to Mazama's commitment to being green. The town's website says, "Our welcoming mountain culture is open minded, adventurous, and good natured," and this seems to be true. Think fly fishing more than bait fishing, nordic skiers outnumbering snowmobilers, birding over hunting—it's more of a quiet outdoor-enthusiast kind of scene. Once you leave State Route 20 and drive through Mazama, you land at the Mazama Store, a tourist attraction unto itself. Stop here for a sandwich before heading out to the swimming hole, especially if you've been biking the North Cascades Highway.

From the informal parking lot, take 100 steps down to the river and you're there. The swimming hole is gorgeous, with crystal-clear green water through which you can see every rock down below. Don't forget to bring your goggles. The water is deep enough for

The Methow Valley is dog- and outdoor-recreationist-friendly.

jumping in and swimming and calm enough for you to effectively use floaties or stand-up paddleboards.

Five or six big boulders dot the river—there's no real cliff jumping, but the boulder jumping is quite delightful. When we were here, a log had been lodged between boulders as a makeshift balance beam. A healthy mix of locals and visitors lounge on the boulders like turtles in the sun. You can walk, wade, or swim over to the other side of the river, where there's a sandy beach that's perfect for building little sand castles and just enjoying nature with your kids or dogs.

In fact, 90 percent of the Methow Valley trails are dog friendly, with summertime opportunities for biking, horseback riding, and birding pre- or post-swim. If you head in the opposite direction from the river toward the cliffs, you'll find some popular rocks to climb. Of course, retrace your steps to go for a swim afterward.

 ## 62 BOULDER CREEK FALLS

TYPE: Mountain-forest creek, waterfall, pools
LOCATION: Roadside in Okanogan–Wenatchee National Forest north of Winthrop via SR 20
WATER: Cold, clear, clean, blue-green
SEASON: Summer into early fall
WHO'S HERE: Recreationists, locals, anglers
AMENITIES: Parking; camping, food, and lodging nearby
LOCAL'S TIP: Love cowboys? Of course you do. Stop in Winthrop to check out the tourist-friendly Wild West theme.
GPS COORDINATES: 48.5792 N, –120.1573 W

GETTING THERE

From State Route 20 in Winthrop, turn north onto Bridge Street. After 0.2 mile, turn right onto Bluff Street. After 0.4 mile, the road name changes to Eastside Chewuch Road. After 5.8 miles, bear right onto unpaved Forest Road 37. After 1.3 miles, turn right to stay on FR 37. After 0.6 mile, park at a big pulloff on the right side of the road.

Boulder Creek flows from the Okanogan–Wenatchee National Forest northeast of Winthrop into the Chewuch River, which flows into the Methow River at Winthrop. Because the Boulder Creek area is not in the main Methow Valley, usually it is less crowded. Boulder Creek is small, with a good-size—around 20-foot-high—waterfall. Come during low flow; this region is drier than the west side of the Cascades, so it should be safe once the main snowmelt has happened.

Every swimming hole is made a little better with a waterfall.

From the parking spot, two options—each about 100 feet long—are clearly visible: You can scramble down a steep hillside downstream of the falls right off the parking spot, but this route is a bit sketchy, with loose dirt and a lack of things to hang onto. The better option is to head upriver to the top of the waterfall; slightly across and uphill from the waterfall there are two distinct trails. Pick your way on either of these down a steep hillside that has more to grab onto, then, as you get closer to the river, work upstream to find a safe spot to wade across. You'll now be on river left. From here, scramble down to below the waterfall.

There are a couple of little pools to swim in and some rocks to lizard out on. This is a sunbather's paradise, with lots of excellent places to hang out beside the river and soak up some sunshine. Rocks and cliff faces loom up on either side of the river, and it feels like the sun is reflecting back and forth between them, a dreamy contrast to the ice-cold water, perfect for doing an ice plunge between sun sessions. This is where most people are hanging out.

You can also swim up to underneath the waterfall to find a bigger pool. It's like being in a cavern, with some rocks to jump off of. However, the water's not superdeep, so be careful. You'll see lots of fishing signs around, so expect to see anglers, although they tend to shy away during the heat of the day, when swimmers are more likely to be here, so it shouldn't be a problem.

 METHOW RIVER SWIMMING HOLE

TYPE: Lowland river, current, eddies, pools, beach
LOCATION: Roadside between Winthrop and Twisp via SR 20

WATER: Cold, clear, clean, blue-green
SEASON: Summer into early fall
WHO'S HERE: Kid-friendly, dog-friendly; everyone
AMENITIES: Parking; food and lodging nearby
LOCAL'S TIP: If you're feeling inspired, volunteer with the Methow Conservancy, which protects and provides access to this swimming hole, or become a conservancy member.
GPS COORDINATES: 48.4164 N, −120.1455 W

GETTING THERE

FROM WINTHROP: Head southeast on State Route 20 for 3.5 miles and turn left onto Old Twisp Highway; after 1.1 miles, arrive at trailhead parking. **FROM SOUTH OF TWISP:** At the junction of SR 20 and SR 153, go north on SR 20 for 5.2 miles, passing through Twisp, and turn right onto Old Twisp Highway. After 1 mile, arrive at trailhead parking.

By partnering with local landowners, the Methow Conservancy works to permanently protect local wildlife, open space, forests, farms, and riverfronts. This swimming hole belongs to that last group, which is part of 12.81 miles of Methow River included in the Winthrop-to-Mazama area easements. A conservancy sign and designated parking mark this trailhead, and as you head down to the river, check out the various signs and follow their directives—you are accessing protected land, so please obey the rules, including the campsite rule: Leave it better than you found it.

Methow River Swimming Hole offers a great eddy and current to play in.

From the trailhead, stick to the 100-foot-long trail, and at the river, walk downstream another 300 feet to a couple of wading pools. You can walk through the little braided channels spread out along the riverbed—if those aren't obvious, then the water is still too high for safe swimming.

A favorite place to swim is at the point where the river takes a hard turn to the left. Typical of such a river feature, this bend forms a big eddy. There are a couple of eddies here, and folks love to get in at the big eddy, move out into the current, then swim against it, like a river's version of a treadmill. You can also let the current whisk you downriver until you're gently pulled, floating, into the eddy and its sandy shore.

The beach is almost fully exposed, which makes it ideal for sunbathing. The flip side, of course, is that there's not a lot of shade, so pack your own if you require protection from the sun. While you're at it, bring your swim goggles, floaties, and an inner tube to ride down this stretch of current.

 ## METHOW RIVER: AT TWISP

TYPE: Lowland river, pool, beach
LOCATION: Roadside near town park in Twisp via SR 20
WATER: Cold, clear, clean, blue-green
SEASON: Summer into early fall
WHO'S HERE: Kid-friendly, dog-friendly; locals
AMENITIES: Parking, restrooms, playground, swimming pool; food and camping nearby
LOCAL'S TIP: Visit the Glover Street Market, named after homesteader Henry C. Glover, for some fresh-pressed juices and smoothies. This natural-food store is so good, we've driven all the way down from the upper part of the Methow Valley just to shop.
GPS COORDINATES: 48.3678 N, –120.1201 W

GETTING THERE

FROM TWISP: On State Route 20 eastbound, just south of the Twisp River turn east onto East Twisp Avenue. FROM SOUTH OF TWISP: At the junction of SR 20 and SR 153, turn northwest onto SR 20, and after 2.6 miles, turn right onto East Twisp Avenue. FROM EITHER DIRECTION: After 0.1 mile turn left onto North Lincoln Street. After 0.2 mile, arrive at a large paved parking area for Twisp Park.

The town of Twisp is not large. It's a laid-back place, with a friendly feel. For a town with such a small population (919 within the 1.2-mile town limits, according to the 2010 census), there are lots of fine restaurants and grocery stores for a post-swim snack. The starting point for this swim is Twisp Park on North Lincoln Street, which is near the

Methow Valley Community Center, not far from the Wagner Memorial Pool. During the summer, Twisp Park comes alive, with children running around the playground and adults sampling honey, perusing pottery, and bagging produce at the Methow Valley Farmers Market.

From the parking lot, walk down an unmarked but well-beaten trail to the riverbed a stone's throw away, then wade across the one or two or three braided channels (the number of channels depends on that year's rainfall). Keep working upstream on river right along the main river (not the braids) for about 500 feet, until you reach a giant pool. It's obvious—you'll know when you get there.

In fact, this pool is so big you can check it out on Google Earth. It is truly like a giant swimming pool—current comes down into it and current leaves it, but the pool itself is big, deep, calm, and blue. It wouldn't surprise us if it's 20 feet or more deep.

The last time we were here, a sandbar had formed, providing a shallow area within the pool to hang out on. (Like the channels, the sandbar's shape and size depend on the river, but it's a good guess that it shows up every year.) The sandbar drops off into the deep end of the pool, where there's plenty of room to lounge on an inner tube and soak up some sun. The large swath of shoreline also has plenty of sunbathing opportunities.

If you're interested in some mellow jumping, swim over to the rock buttress on river left. This rocky wall protrudes into the swimming hole, giving you a 5-foot-high, max, ledge from which to jump. Once you're done swimming, check out the town.

Methow Valley goodness right in the town of Twisp

So many cliffs, so much time (Swim #66)

BELLINGHAM AREA AND NORTH

BELLINGHAM, A SMALL CITY in Whatcom County, is home to Western Washington University. Just 21 miles south of the Canada–US border, Bellingham is known for its green style and enthusiasm for outdoor recreation, demonstrated by its more than 60 miles of bike lanes and nearly 70 miles of trails. The main river in this chapter, the Nooksack, flows off Mount Baker to the east, a Cascades peak that's a favorite playground for Bellinghamsters and other Pacific Northwesterners in summer and winter.

 ## 65 BELLINGHAM BAY: LUMMI ISLAND

TYPE: Saltwater, currents, tides, beach
LOCATION: Boat-in on southeast shore of Lummi Island via I-5 north of Bellingham
WATER: Cold, clearish, cleanish, dark blue-green
SEASON: Late spring through early fall
WHO'S HERE: Expert kayakers and canoers, campers; likely just you and your people
AMENITIES: DIY campsite, picnic table; campsites and outhouses nearby (Lummi Island Campground)
NOTE: Permit required for optional crabbing
LOCAL'S TIP: Bellingham's six craft-beer breweries have won the town recognition as one of the best beer cities in the United States. Stop by for a cold one on your way out.
GPS COORDINATES: 48.6805 N, –122.6315 W (parking); 48.6600 N, –122.6140 W (unnamed cove); 48.6588 N, –122.6143 W (Lummi Island Campground)

An epic voyage for the expert kayaker (photo by Daniel Roche)

GETTING THERE

From I-5 north of Bellingham, take exit 260 and drive west on Slater Road 4 miles, then turn left onto Haxton Way and follow it southwest 6.7 miles to the Whatcom County Ferry Terminal on Gooseberry Point; park for free on the other side of Lummi View Drive. From here you have two options. **FOR A SHORTER PADDLE:** Drive onto Lummi Island via the ferry, turn left (south) onto South Nugent Road, and follow it 0.5 mile to Seacrest Drive. Turn left onto Seacrest and follow it south (the name changes to Beach Avenue) 3.2 miles to Smugglers Cove, then put your boat in the water here. **FOR A LONGER PADDLE:** Put your boat in at the gravel beach next to the Whatcom County Ferry Terminal, paddle straight across Hale Passage roughly 1 mile, then paddle down the Lummi east shoreline south approximately 5 miles to the large, protected, unnamed cove.

One of our favorite swimming spots is a secret little campground on Lummi Island, accessible only by water. But it's not for the novice—in order to get here, you have to kayak or canoe across Hale Passage, which, like most bodies of water associated with the ocean, is subject to currents, tides, and weather. Be sure you're well prepared before making the trip. This is a pack-it-in, pack-it-out destination, so bring everything, plus bags to carry out your garbage with you when you go. Don't forget to bring water! If you have a seaworthy vessel and the skills to operate it, this spot is totally worth the effort.

Once you cross the passage and head south along the southeastern shore of Lummi, you pass (or start from) Smugglers Cove and come to Inati Bay. Make a shore stop at Inati Bay (campsites, outhouses, picnic tables) for some excellent big-rock cliff jumping.

Continue south past the next little cove (Reil Harbor) and its large rocky outcropping, then land at a large, protected, unnamed cove that has one campsite and picnic table.

From the beach some trails lead into the woods; if you walk 500 feet south, you come to a larger cove—Lummi Island Campground, which is big enough for larger boats—that has more campsites and some pit toilets. As you wander the shore, pick up one of

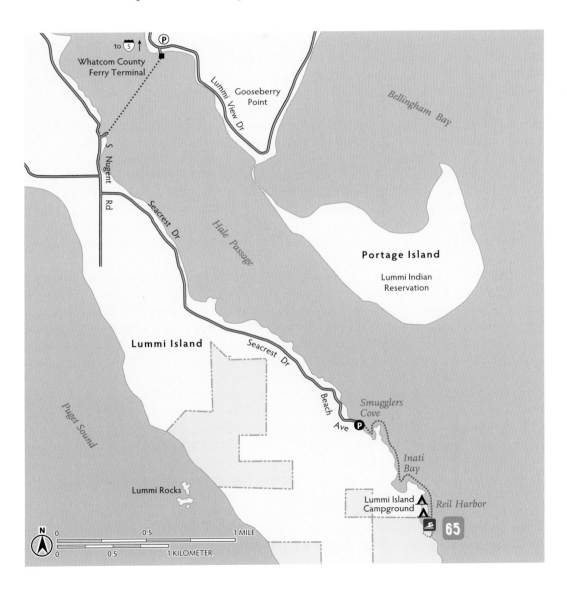

the many flat Lummi beach rocks—they make a great platter for charcuterie and fancy cheeses you might be picnicking on. Just remember to leave them behind—rinsed off— when you head home.

The waters off Lummi feature an extra bonus: phosphorescence, which occurs when certain kinds of plankton emit light, usually as a response to touch. Usually this light is diffuse, glowing, and fleeting. But sometimes the phosphorescence has a different jam going on, like fireflies swarming around in the water. When that happens, each step you take in the shallows lights up large and discrete neon specks for a few seconds before the water fades back into blackness. Taking a nighttime swim with goggles in phosphorescence is just like those scenes in *Star Trek* when Captain Jean-Luc Picard says, "Engage" and then all the stars turn into long streaks of light zipping by at light speed. One of the best things about phosphorescence, aside from the fact that it's mind-blowingly cool, is that its image is nearly impossible to capture on any sort of device. It's dim, so your eyes have to adjust to see it, and it never lasts long enough to catch on camera. You can really only experience it in person.

In the mornings, the beach at either camp spot provides a cozy little nook for coffee and breakfast. Facing east, they both catch the sun just right, so you get warmed up before throwing on your kit and heading out for a day of swimming and diving around the various coves and rocky outcroppings that dot the coastline. In season, there's crab to hunt, if you don't mind risking a pinch (and permits are dutifully acquired), and lots of other cool sea life to check out.

You might luck out and find a DIY sauna—or you can build your own, if you bring the necessary hand tools, such as a hatchet and a hand auger. Construct it out of driftwood lashed together with kelp and cover it with blankets and dried seaweed for insulation, then heat rocks in a big campfire. Once the rocks are hot, put them in the sauna and sprinkle them with saltwater to get it nice and steamy. Really, there's nothing better than running back and forth between the dang-cold ocean and a toasty seawater-misted homemade sauna.

You can also bushwhack up to a steep, rocky outcropping behind the unnamed cove's campsite. Here, about 100 feet above the water, is a grove of a half dozen or so sturdy madrona trees. At this writing, a network of hammocks made from fishing nets, ropes, and driftwood were strung between these trees about 20 feet up. Judging from the condition of the ropes, this ideal nap zone has likely been hanging for a while, so be sure to check the sturdiness of the hammocks before getting in them.

When it's time to head home, return the way you came—or, if you're an experienced seafarer, take a scenic detour clockwise around the island: Paddle south around the tip of the island and north up to the Lummi Rocks, where you can land your boat for lunch. Then continue north up and around the island's north end—10 to 15 miles starting from the unnamed cove's campsite (depending on your route)—before striking out across Hale Passage back to the mainland at Gooseberry Point.

66 WHATCOM CREEK: WHATCOM FALLS PARK

TYPE: Lowland creek, pool, cliff jump
LOCATION: Short walk or hike-in in city park in Bellingham via I-5
WATER: Cold to cool, clearish, cleanish, blue-green
SEASON: Summer into fall
WHO'S HERE: Kid-friendly, leashed-dog-friendly; everyone
AMENITIES: Parking, restrooms, picnic tables and shelters, grills, playgrounds, tennis courts, basketball court, multipurpose fields; food and lodging nearby
LOCAL'S TIP: After your swim, stop by one of the many excellent restaurants and bars in B-ham.
GPS COORDINATES: 48.7512 N, −122.4289 W

GETTING THERE

From I-5 in Bellingham, take exit 253 to Lakeway Drive eastbound. Stay on Lakeway Drive for around 1.5 miles, then turn left onto Silver Beach Road into Whatcom Falls Park. Continue past Arbor Court to the parking lot on the right. Follow park trails either 900 feet or 0.4 mile (elevation loss: 100 feet; high point: about 200 feet).
BY BUS: From the downtown Bellingham station, take Whatcom Transit Authority bus No. 512 to Roland Street. Walk across Lakeway Drive and follow Silver Beach Road about 0.5 mile to the parking area.

Right smack-dab in the town of Bellingham, Whatcom Falls Park is a popular, social spot. Here's where you go if you want to be with people, certainly not if you're looking for any kind of wilderness or remoteness. Since it's an in-town park, there are lots of folks just cruising by. Some stop for a dip, others walk the many trails. Whatcom Creek is a fun stream winding through the park, pouring over several small falls and ledges before eventually flowing through downtown and into Bellingham Bay. For those who live in the area, this park is akin to the local public bathhouse—so easy to get to and so fun to hang out at that many come here every day during the summer for that rejuvenating submersion. In short, if you love people-watching and convenience, this is the place for you. All in all, this park has an easy-to-access location, great cliff jumping, and good vibes. If every town had a community swimming hole such as Bellingham's Whatcom Falls Park, the world would be a better place.

From the parking lot, walk northwest down the main trail to a bridge over Whatcom Falls. Once across the creek, about 450 feet from the parking lot, you reach a trail junction, where you have a couple of options.

If you turn right and walk upstream another 450 feet, you'll reach a point where the trail and river get very close and a bedrock shelf juts out into a nice pool—nice, but secondary to the main attraction farther downstream (see below). Here, above this pool, an approximately

5-foot waterfall is formed by a stone ledge that you can climb around on and potentially jump off if you find a deep entry spot. A log beside the pool also provides obstacle-course opportunities. This is a quieter, smaller play area that might be better for the little ones.

To get to the main swimming attraction downstream, after crossing the bridge over the creek, take a left and follow the main trail that parallels the creek on river right for about 0.3 mile, losing roughly 100 feet of elevation. Leave the trail near the upstream end of the featured swimming hole, walking about 140 feet to the downstream end of the pool. It's like a giant swimming pool in the forest, and the sides have some man-made structure to them. There are areas shaded by big trees as well as zones that get hit by plenty of sun. The downstream end of the pool on river right is the shallow end, where kids and their caregivers wade and splash about. The other side has two big cliff jumps, and this side tends to attract high schoolers and the college crowd.

Here's where you might want to remember what your own caregiver of yore asked: "If everyone jumped off a bridge, would you?" Same goes for cliff jumps. The water is not totally clear and so the bottom is not visible—which means you can't know for certain what the hazards lurking below may be. Check the depth for yourself before jumping, and understand the risks of jumping into unknown water before taking the leap. That said, it's pretty awesome cliff jumping.

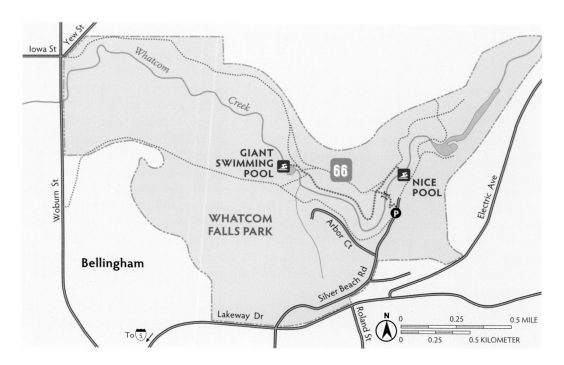

The Whatcom Falls Park cliff jump

67 SOUTH FORK NOOKSACK RIVER: TUBING ZONE

TYPE: Lowland river, slow current, beach
LOCATION: Roadside east of Bellingham via I-5 and SR 542
WATER: Cold to cool, clearish, cleanish, blue-green
SEASON: Summer into early fall
WHO'S HERE: Kid-friendly, dog-friendly; college and high school kids, families
AMENITIES: Food and lodging nearby
LOCAL'S TIP: Take your bike to shuttle back to your car, so you won't need two cars.
GPS COORDINATES: 48.7187 N, −122.2031 W

GETTING THERE

From I-5 in Bellingham, take exit 255 onto State Route 542 east and drive 14.6 miles just past Deming to SR 9. Turn south onto SR 9 and drive 7.1 miles, to just across the South Fork Nooksack River outside the hamlet of Acme; turn left into a signed lot (room for ten or twelve cars) and park.

What more do you need?

Right outside Bellingham, there are multiple places to pull over and park alongside the South Fork Nooksack River. The river here is very calm, with just enough current to keep it fresh and clean despite being pretty low in the drainage, and it has a nice beach. You may find other impromptu parking spots, but please be respectful of private property, and only get into the water at public access points.

From the parking lot, follow the trail 100 feet or so down to the beach, where you can set up a sun tent or lawn chair for a lazy day of lounging in the sun. Stay here all day, getting in and out of the water at your leisure, or just pop in for a quick refresh on your day.

You could bring your inner tube—this is clearly a spot where tubers launch. During the height of summer, the water level might be too low and with very little current, so expect the tubing to be slow. As always, when tubing you should have an idea of your exit strategy. There's one exit point about 0.7 mile downstream, not far around the river bend, which is close enough you wouldn't even need to drop off a car or bike first for a shuttle back to where you started—or if you have a runner in the group, make sure he or she takes shoes with them when they tube. While this might sound like a short distance, tubes move slow, so embrace the slow living and do two laps if you need more.

The current is superslow, and once you go past this exit point, you won't have a lot of exit options for a couple miles, which commits you to a longer tubing session. Be prepared to go the distance, because it'll be a while, and you never know when wind might hit and slow you down even more. Put that zinc sunblock on your nose and bring some water—you don't want to be one of those dehydrated (and drunk) sunburnt people staggering to shore at the end of the day.

 ## 68 RACEHORSE CREEK FALLS

TYPE: Lowland-forest creek, waterfall, pools
LOCATION: Hike-in in Mount Baker–Snoqualmie National Forest east of Bellingham via I-5 and SR 542
WATER: Cold to cool, clear, clean, blue-green
SEASON: Summer into early fall
WHO'S HERE: College students, Bellingham locals
AMENITIES: Food and lodging nearby
LOCAL'S TIP: In 2009 a giant landslide at the base of Mount Baker exposed sandstone beds that contain 50-million-year-old fossils, including a large fossilized palm frond. To explore the Racehorse Falls fossil fields, contact paleontologist George Mustoe at Western Washington University (mustoeg@wwu.edu).
GPS COORDINATES: 48.8826 N, –122.1313 W (parking); 48.8789 N, –122.1252 W (swimming hole)

GETTING THERE

From I-5 in Bellingham, take exit 255 onto State Route 542 east and follow it 16.9 miles, then turn right onto Mosquito Lake Road. After 0.9 mile, turn left on North Fork Road. After 4.2 miles, turn right onto an unmarked and unnamed road just before crossing Racehorse Creek. Drive about 0.25 mile, looking for a pullout on the right near an unmarked but obvious trail on the left (elevation gain: 150 feet; high point: 600 feet).

Racehorse is a small creek, and it requires a lot of rain to get high water levels. You might even be able to go earlier in the season than you would at bigger rivers, even as early as late May or the beginning of June, as long as spring hasn't brought too much precipitation. Every now and then, a kayaker braves Racehorse Creek Falls at its highest volume. That's how we first found out about this area and decided to check it out for swimming purposes. We're very glad we did. Ten miles from Bellingham, Racehorse Creek Falls is a local favorite.

From where you parked, cross the road to the obvious trail and follow it through the forest for about 0.1 mile to the riverbed. You could stop here—some folks hang out in these shallows before the falls, building their own little pools with rocks and generally just having fun playing around in the mellow part of the creek. Check out this zone if you have younger kids.

During the summer, hike about another 0.25 mile upstream via the stream channel, which will be nearly dried up and easy to traverse. If there is any more than a small

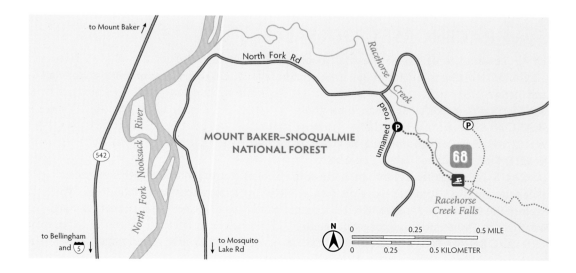

Waterfalls are cool.

amount of water in the channel, and certainly if it is difficult to hike through the channel, there will be too much water in the creek for swimming below the falls.

Just before you get to the base of the falls, you have to climb over and find your way through some boulders. This is a popular spot, so there are likely some well-traveled routes through this zone. You'll hear the falls just as you see them.

The waterfall is a decent size, 139 feet from top to bottom and divided into four sections, with three "punchbowl" swimming holes. On a hot-weather weekend, you'll run into college students and their buddies sunbathing, cooling off in the water, or even sliding down the rock face. Earlier in the day is best, not only because that's when it's likely to be less crowded, but also because that's when you get the best sun. Try the couple hours before sunset as well—within the narrow canyon, light can get in only during short windows of the day.

The biggest pool is the one at the bottom. The final stretch of waterfall that drops into this pool isn't at a straight vertical; rather, it slides down along the rock, made of Chuckanut sandstone. This isn't a cliff-jumping destination so much as potentially a rock-sliding one, though it's quite a steep angle, and this rock face alone is a noteworthy feature. By the time the water gets to this pool, it is fairly calm. On either side, trees tower, ferns sway in the breeze, and moss drips, creating a green Northwest oasis.

So Northwest (Swim #68)

RESOURCES

NATIONAL PARKS

Mount Rainier National Park
55210 238th Avenue East
Ashford, WA 98304
(360) 569-6575
www.nps.gov/mora/index.htm

North Cascades National Park
810 State Route 20
Sedro-Woolley, WA 98284
(360) 854-7200
www.nps.gov/noca/index.htm

Olympic National Park
Visitor Center
3002 Mount Angeles Road
Port Angeles, WA 98362
(360) 565-3130
www.nps.gov/olym/index.htm

NATIONAL FORESTS

Gifford-Pinchot National Forest
Fort Vancouver Visitor Center
1501 East Evergreen Boulevard
Vancouver, WA 98661
(360) 891-5000
www.fs.usda.gov/gifford
pinchot/

Mount Baker–Snoqualmie National Forest
2930 Wetmore Avenue, Suite 3A
Everett, WA, 98201
(425) 783-6000
www.fs.usda.gov/mbs

Okanogan–Wenatchee National Forest
215 Melody Lane
Wenatchee, WA 98801
(509) 664-9200
www.fs.usda.gov/okawen/

Olympic National Forest
Supervisor's Office
1835 Black Lake Boulevard SW
Olympia, WA 98512
(360) 956-2402
www.fs.usda.gov/olympic/

MOUNTAIN BIKING

Evergreen Mountain Bike Alliance
www.evergreenmtb.org

Mountain Bike Project
www.mtbproject.com

PASSES

Discover Pass
(866) 320-9933
www.discoverpass.wa.gov

Northwest Forest Pass
(800) 270-7504
www.fs.usda.gov/detail/r6
/passes-permits/recreation

RIVER FLOWS

American Whitewater, Washington State Rivers
www.americanwhitewater.org
/content/River/state-summary
/state/WA/

USGS streamflow information
https://waterdata.usgs.gov/wa
/nwis/rt

TRAIL ORGANIZATIONS

All Trails
www.alltrails.com

Mountain Hub
https://mountainhub.com
/explore?feed=map

The Mountaineers
www.mountaineers.org

Washington Trails Association
www.wta.org

YOU'LL WANT THESE

Anacortes Community Forest Lands
904 6th Street
Anacortes, WA 98221
(360) 293-1918
www.cityofanacortes.org
/517/Community
-Forest-Lands-ACFL

Burke Museum of National History and Culture
PO Box 353010
Seattle, WA 98195
(206) 616-3962
www.burkemuseum.org

Columbia River Gorge Natural Scenic Area
902 Wasco Avenue, Suite 200
Hood River, OR 97031
(541) 308-1700
www.fs.usda.gov/main/crgnsa
/home

Duwamish Longhouse and Cultural Center
4705 West Marginal Way SW
Seattle, WA 98106
(206) 431-1582
duwamishtribe.org

Leave No Trace
www.lnt.org

Mountain Project
www.mountainproject.com

Swimming Holes of Washington Instagram
www.instagram.com
/swimmingholesofwashington

INDEX

ACKNOWLEDGMENTS

THANK YOU TO Jeremy Faber for your infinite knowledge about the backwoods of Washington, especially the obscure roads like Toats Coulee Road. Thank you to Tom Barwick of Barwick Photography for always being generous with your photos and secret spots.

Thank you to Ingrid Emerick, Leslie Miller, and everyone at Girl Friday Productions for your support of this project.

Thank you, Jenna Land Free and Andrea Dunlop, for your expert guidance on the proposal.

Thank you to Greg Dick, Matt Dillon, Christopher Matthias, Daryl McDonald, Kristin Mehus-Roe, Hilary Neevel, Daniel Roche, Chris Tretwald, Martin and Gina Volken, and Zac West for your intel, writing, and photo contributions.

Thank you, Kate Rogers, Mary Metz, and the Mountaineers Books team. Thanks to Kris Fulsaas, Lynn Greisz, and Laura Case Larson for your superb editorial contributions. Thank you, Heidi Smets, for the beautiful design and also Ben Pease for the illuminating maps.

Thank you Huxley el Jefe, Bonnie Katz Brindle, and Herschel K. Lucias for your emotional support.

And special thanks to Troy Lucero and Jen Daniels for your patience, modeling, copiloting, and support in this project and for all the other ways you made this book happen.

ABOUT THE AUTHORS

ANNA KATZ is a writer and editor. She lives with her husband and dogs in Seattle. You can find her at helloannakatz.com.

SHANE ROBINSON is an American Mountain Guides Association (AMGA) ski guide in the winter and a tree house builder the rest of the year. He has been exploring the mountains, rivers, and forests of the Cascades ever since he moved to Seattle with his wife in 2002. See more of his exploits on Instagram @shanecrobinson.

ABOUT SKIPSTONE

Skipstone guides explore healthy lifestyles, backyard activism, and how an outdoor life relates to the well-being of our planet. Sustainable foods and gardens; healthful living; realistic and doable conservation at home; modern aspirations for community—Skipstone tries to address such topics in ways that emphasize active living, local and grassroots practices, and a small footprint. Our hope is that Skipstone books will inspire you to celebrate the freedom and generosity of a life outdoors.

All of our publications, as part of our 501(c)(3) nonprofit program, are made possible through the generosity of donors and through sales of more than 800 titles on outdoor recreation, sustainable lifestyle, and conservation. To donate, purchase books, or learn more, visit us online:

SKIPSTONE

LIVE LIFE

MAKE RIPPLES

www.skipstonebooks.org
www.mountaineersbooks.org

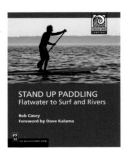

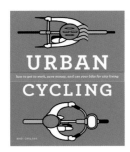

Leave No Trace strives to educate visitors about the nature of their recreational impacts and offers techniques to prevent and minimize such impacts. Leave No Trace is best understood as an educational and ethical program, not as a set of rules and regulations. For more information, visit www.lnt.org or call 800-332-4100.